MAKE & FREEZE

The ultimate guide to family-friendly meal prep

Lou Robbie

Photography by **Ella Miller**

DEDICATION

This book is dedicated to my dad and my sister Siobhán, both taken too soon. Growing up, dinners around the table were always hectic with our family of eight, but there was always so much fun and laughter. If I had them back for a day I'd cook them the most amazing meal. xx

Contents

Introduction — 6

CHAPTER 1.
Breakfast — 18

CHAPTER 2.
Savoury Lunchboxes — 40

CHAPTER 3.
Sweet Lunchboxes — 60

CHAPTER 4.
Soups & Smoothies — 82

CHAPTER 5.
Slow Cooker Dinners — 100

CHAPTER 6.
Air Fryer — 122

CHAPTER 7.
Family Pies & Delicious Dishes — 144

CHAPTER 8.
Better-than-Shop-bought Treats — 168

CHAPTER 9.
Bread — 192

CHAPTER 10.
Sneaky Sweet Stuff — 216

Meal Plans — 238
Thanks — 246
Index — 249

A little bit about me

I am **Lou**, I'm a professional chef, and a proud wife to Mike, my tall Scottish rock of support, and mum to Meabh, aged ten, who is sharp, witty and so kind, and Hamish, aged seven, who is strong-willed, constantly curious and so funny. They are my whole world.

When my Meabh was one, I remember cooking for her and thinking how fortunate I was to have trained as a chef and to have learned the skills needed to feed her real, wholesome homemade food. I made all her purées, finger foods, sauces and weaning dinners from scratch right from the start. I clearly remember feeling the urge to help other parents find the confidence to do the same. This book is both for confident cooks and for those just starting out. If you are starting out, remember that cooking is a skill that can be learned at any age, it just takes practice.

When we cook food from scratch for our families, we are in control of the ingredients. In a world of convenience and processed foods that's a powerful thing.

My food story

I have always been a lover of food. I was the child who licked the plate clean. I grew up in rural Ireland in the 80s, one of six children, in a household where daily mealtimes were structured and the weekly menu was predictable. We'd have potatoes seven days a week, with a combination of mince, bacon and cabbage, beef stew, fish on Fridays and a roast chicken on a Sunday. My mother baked brown bread, apple tarts and sponge cakes from scratch. Treats and chocolates were rare, and my school lunch was always a cheese or ham-and-cheese sandwich on white bread. Irish food was basic but wholesome, and not influenced much by other world cuisines.

As I got older, I tried lots of new foods and enjoyed exploring all tastes. In my twenties I went travelling and that opened up the world of food and flavours even more. I backpacked and ate my way around the food markets of Asia, taking in the sights and sounds and smells. One outstanding memory was of an incredible giant fish platter we ordered from a little beach shack on the stunning island of Koh Phi Phi in Thailand. The fish was cooked in front of us on hot coals and the platter was made up of huge mussels, massive prawns and whole grilled fish – it was a real feast for the eyes and soul.

Introduction

Becoming a chef

After spending a couple of years in Australia and New Zealand, I returned home to find that Ireland had really changed – it was now a diverse, multicultural mecca with a whole new and exciting food scene. And after many years spent working in hospitality I decided to go back to college and train to be a chef, and with that my love of food really flourished.

At college we were taught the French classics: béchamel sauce, boeuf bourguignon, tarte tatin. I learned the art of making food and gained an appreciation of the time taken to layer flavours, and to apply basic techniques like cooking an onion until sweet at the start of making a soup, or searing beef on a high heat for a stew, both of which give depth of flavour to the completed dish.

I put my training into practice and worked in professional kitchens in Galway for over ten years. As a professional chef I had to plan and prepare food every day, write weekly menus, order produce and cook seasonally. All of this I then applied to my cooking at home.

Introduction

Introduction

Growing a global audience of more than 1 million followers

When the pandemic happened, I found myself at home, cooking for my family, and I adapted all the skills I'd learned in the professional kitchen to my home kitchen. Wanting to share these skills with others, I started giving online cooking classes to adults and kids, and set up my business, Little Lou Cooks, in 2021. I also began sharing recipes and meal-prepping tips on my social media pages and the momentum grew, as more and more parents were interested in swapping shop-bought meals for healthier homemade food that could be made in advance. In November 2023 I shared a video of me doing what I do – batch-making homemade snacks suitable for freezing for my kids' school lunches – and it went viral! That snowballed and now I have over 1 million followers across my social media platforms.

I love that I have a global community of followers who are so supportive and encouraging – thank you so much for helping me get this far. Most are parents, who send me the loveliest comments, photos and messages daily. I get to work from home and really feel I am helping parents to add more homemade food to their weekly menus. I always encourage everyone to make use of their freezer, to cook extra and save some for another day, for when you're under pressure but still want your family to eat good homemade food.

The road to my first cookbook

I really love the warm and encouraging support from my online community. But when my page grew so rapidly, I wanted to get my recipes into a book. The online world is fast, sometimes fleeting and fluid, but a book is peaceful, tangible and timeless. A book can be loved and used and passed on. This book is for you to continue your food journey with your kids.

Make this your handbook as your kids make their way through school: scribble on it, make notes, and earmark the favourites. You never know, they might make those recipes for their own kids one day.

Introduction

Sarah 1w

From the mum of a super-fussy eater who loves a whole heap of your lunchbox ideas. He's eating dates. And sweet potato. Thank you!

Avril 1w

Kids said 'delicious' so I'll take that! Also made a freezer stock of apple and date bars. Thanks for all your effort.

Jennifer 3w

Hi there! I just wanted to say thanks for your school lunchbox recipes and the stew one too! We're all well fed here today. The kids helped bake over mid-term, so we had lovely family time too. I was buying flapjacks and pancakes but now we're stocked up for a few weeks of delicious home-made snacks and I know exactly what's in them!

Charlotte 1w

Made a few of your muffin recipes and my 4 and 1-year-old love them! Helps me feel so organised and happier knowing what's in what they are eating.

Jenny 2w

Hello, just wanted to say thank you for putting your recipes on here. I have made so many things especially for the kids' packed lunches. I can't tell you how many peanut butter chocolate cups I have made! Even my husband gets excited by them. Looking to try the chocolate and beetroot combo soon! xxx

Rachel 1w

Just wanted to say thank you. I've filled my freezer today with mini scones, easy oat bars and ABC muffins ready for next half-term. Super-easy recipes and my son had a great time helping me. Thanks so much!

What you'll find in the book

Breakfast can be more exciting than cereal – add colour with compotes and fresh fruit, make homemade pancakes and potato waffles, and add veggies and sauces.

Lunchbox fillers . . . sweet and savoury, portioned, portable and never boring.

Dinners, handy **air-fryer** favourites, **slow-cooker** heroes and **family pies and delicious dishes**.

Soups and smoothies are sometimes the easiest way to sneak in the good stuff.

Better-than-shop-bought treats – fun to make, delicious to eat and guilt-free too.

Sneaky sweet stuff – add vegetables and pulses to your sweet bakes and see if anyone notices!

Bread of all sorts for all levels of baker, and all great for the lunchbox.

Love your freezer, don't fear it!

The freezer can be a home cook's best friend. Embrace it and use it to save yourself precious time in the future.

Size isn't everything. We don't need massive freezers. It's more important that you utilize what you have and that the food you choose to freeze is on rotation. That way there is less waste.

The key to freezer success

CLEAN IT OUT
It's the best way of getting to know what's in there. Discard any food items that are past their use-by date. Remove all the ice, clean it and you're ready to start afresh.

MAKE A LIST
Write a list of everything on a piece of paper or whiteboard, and keep it on the freezer door or in a handy place so you can add to it and cross off things as they get used.

LABEL AND DATE
It's very important that cooked food is cool before it is stored in the fridge or freezer. Once cooled, store it properly and clearly label and date it with a permanent marker.

STORAGE BAGS
I like to use freezer-safe reusable bags or ziplock bags. They take up less space than containers and they can be laid flat.

STORAGE CONTAINERS
Plastic and glass containers are fine, but use the appropriate size, because if the container is too big, freezer burn will form.

REMOVE THE AIR
This helps to avoid freezer burn. Items freeze better when the air is removed, so try to expel as much air as possible before closing the bags or containers.

HOW LONG CAN I FREEZE IT FOR?
The guidelines are 3 months in a shallow freezer/standing freezer and 6 months in a deep freezer.

DEFROSTING
Best practice is to defrost high-risk foods on a plate in the fridge overnight – generally these are foods containing meat or dairy. Baked goods are usually low-risk foods that can defrost in a container on the worktop within 1-2 hours or overnight.

COOK FROM FROZEN
It is possible to cook some food from frozen – just make sure the food is reheated to a safe temperature and is piping hot all the way through. It should be 70°C or over when it's safe to serve.

Final tips for getting organized

1. Utilizing your freezer and meal planning are the keys to success when it comes to feeding your kids!

2. Plan the meals for the week just like a chef would do in a restaurant, and write a menu.

3. The weekly menu will dictate everything: the shopping list, the amount of prep for the week and the amount of money you will fork out on the week's food.

4. Include breakfast, lunch, dinner and snacks for 7 days. Flick through each category in the book for inspiration.

5. Keep your weekly meal plans so you can use them again.

6. Decide when you have time to cook, and plan the meals accordingly. For example, you can:

   → Mark the days when you will make pancakes for breakfast and bake bread for lunch. Include any prepared food you have in the freezer for busy days.

   → Plan for easy slow-cooker dinners during the week, pie days when you have a bit more time, and even the perfect Friday night fakeaway using the air fryer.

   → Saturday might be a great day to bake, and Sunday could be your day to prepare and make lunchbox snacks for the busy week ahead.

7. And don't forget to get your kids involved! Let them choose a recipe to make weekly, start with something easy like a muffin or pancake recipe. Give them ownership of it, teach and encourage them in the kitchen. Cooking is such an important life skill and creates the best childhood memories.

Chapter 1

Breakfast

Breakfast

We are a family of pancake lovers. We love every shape and size, we love them during the busy school week and at the weekend too. But to keep things exciting we make many different kinds.

Thin crêpe pancakes are a favourite to make because you can fill them with your favourite flavours. Homemade raspberry chia jam is always popular, but we love savoury too. Try adding slices of ham and grated cheese folded and toasted – they make a delicious breakfast or lunch. Feta and wilted spinach makes another good savoury version.

Crêpes with raspberry chia seed jam

MAKES 8

FOR THE PANCAKES
200ml full-fat milk
110ml water
2 large eggs
150g plain flour
30g butter, melted (I use salted butter)
oil for cooking

FOR THE JAM
350g frozen raspberries
1 teaspoon vanilla extract
2 tablespoons honey (add more if you like)
30g chia seeds (milled or whole)
1 tablespoon lemon juice (optional)

1. To make the batter, measure the milk and water into a jug, then crack in the eggs and whisk to combine. Measure the flour into a mixing bowl, pour in the milk mix and whisk really well. Cover the bowl with a clean towel and leave the batter to rest for 30 minutes. After this time stir in the melted butter.

2. Heat a crêpe-maker or a non-stick frying pan on a medium heat. Drizzle on some oil and wipe with kitchen paper to coat evenly, being careful not to burn your fingers.

3. Add a ladle of the batter and spread it out using a spatula, or if using a pan swirl it quickly. Cook for 2 minutes, then flip and cook for another few minutes. The pancakes should have brown freckles. Repeat.

FOR THE RASPBERRY CHIA SEED JAM

Put the raspberries into a medium pot. Place on the hob and warm on a medium heat, stirring with a wooden spoon. Once the berries are completely soft and heated the whole way through, add the vanilla and honey and stir. Take off the heat and blend. Stir in the chia seeds and lemon juice. Once cool, pour into a spotlessly clean jar.

STORAGE:
This jam keeps for 1 week in the fridge.

TO FREEZE:
Allow the crêpes to cool completely, then layer them between separate squares of baking parchment and place them in a large labelled ziplock bag.

The jam will keep for up to 3 months in the freezer.

TO DEFROST:
Take however many crêpes you need and defrost them overnight in the fridge. Warm them through in a warm dry pan and add your favourite toppings. If you need them in a hurry, heat them through for 30 seconds in the microwave and use as you wish.

Prep time. **15 mins**   Cook time. **25 mins plus resting**

Breakfast

If you love a stack of pancakes, these are for you. I worked for eight years in the most fabulous family café and every weekend we would make hundreds of these pancakes to serve for brunch. You could order a short stack (2 pancakes) or a tall stack (4 pancakes) and add bacon, fruit compote or even both. Just make sure the bacon is crispy and the maple syrup is plentiful!

American-style 'weekend' pancakes with maple & bacon

MAKES 12

2 tablespoons butter, melted
250g self-raising flour
2 tablespoons soft light brown sugar
1 flat teaspoon bicarbonate of soda
270ml milk, a little more if needed
1 egg, at room temperature
1 teaspoon vanilla extract
1 tablespoon vinegar or lemon juice
oil, for cooking
crispy bacon and maple syrup, to serve

1. Put the bacon on to cook in the oven or in the air fryer.
2. Melt the butter in the microwave for about 20–30 seconds and set to one side to cool. Sieve the flour, light brown sugar and bicarbonate of soda into a mixing bowl and stir to combine. Measure the milk, egg, vanilla and vinegar into a jug and whisk with a fork.
3. Make a well in the flour and pour in the milk mix. Gently stir the batter, using the fork, then pour in the melted butter and give it a final mix. The batter will be lumpy, but that's OK. The consistency of the batter is really important. You should be able to pour it, but it should not be too runny. Test it by letting the batter run off the end of the spoon. If it is too thick, add a bit more milk. If it is too runny, add a bit more flour.
4. Put a non-stick frying pan on a medium heat and set the bowl of batter to one side to rest for a couple of minutes. When the pan is heated, add a small bit of oil to coat. Add about 2 tablespoons of the batter to the pan, letting the batter fall off the tip of the spoon. Use the back of the spoon to make the pancake round. Let it cook and brown until bubbles form – this will take a couple of minutes. Then flip and cook for about 1 minute.

 TO FREEZE:
Allow the pancakes to cool completely, then lay them on a tray that will fit into your freezer. Once frozen, remove the tray from the freezer and place the pancakes in a labelled ziplock bag.

 TO DEFROST:
Take however many pancakes you need and defrost them overnight in the fridge. Reheat them in the toaster or in the microwave.

5. Repeat with the rest of the batter. Lay the cooked pancakes on a big baking tray or plate – do not overlap or stack them before you're ready to serve or they will get soggy.

6. Serve with crispy bacon and maple syrup.

Breakfast

There was a time when I thought it was impossible to whip up healthy pancakes on a busy school morning. Then one day I pulled out my smoothie blender and came up with these simple nutritious pancakes, and I haven't looked back! If you're organized, you can put all the ingredients into the blender jug the night before. Then simply blend and cook fresh in the morning. Of course, if you are even more super-organized you can make and freeze them, ready to defrost for any hectic morning.

'School morning' blender pancakes

MAKES 12 SMALL PANCAKES

100g oats
1 ripe banana or 1 peeled and sliced apple
2 eggs
½ teaspoon baking powder
3–4 tablespoons milk
oil, for cooking

1. Measure all the ingredients into a small powerful blender. Blend on high until smooth.
2. Warm a frying pan on a medium heat. Lightly coat the pan with oil, add a tablespoon of the batter, cook until bubbles form, then flip and cook for a further minute. Serve with yoghurt, fruit and maple syrup.

STORAGE:
Store in an airtight container in the fridge for up to 3 days.

TO FREEZE:
Allow the pancakes to cool completely, then lay them on a tray that will fit into your freezer. Once frozen, remove the tray from the freezer and place the pancakes in a labelled ziplock bag.

TO DEFROST:
Take the number of pancakes you need and defrost them overnight in the fridge. Heat them in the toaster, in a warm frying pan or in the microwave.

TIP:
I use my smoothie blender for these pancakes. You can measure everything into the jug the night before and store it in the fridge, ready to blend in the morning. Don't blend it the night before, because the mix will get too thick.

Prep time. **5 mins**   Cook time. **15 mins**

I remember the first time I baked oats it was during lockdown and we were all baking like crazy. I made a similar version to these and couldn't believe how good they tasted. I like to bake them as a traybake, using baking parchment so you can lift them out, portion and freeze some for another day. My kids love this for breakfast. It's a real treat with lots of goodness added.

Chocolate & banana baked oats

MAKES 6 PORTIONS

200g rolled oats
40g pumpkin/sunflower seeds (optional)
25g chocolate chips or raisins
3 tablespoons cocoa powder
1 flat teaspoon ground cinnamon
1½ teaspoons baking powder
300ml milk of your choice
2 eggs
1 tablespoon runny honey
1 ripe banana, mashed, or 1 apple, peeled and grated
yoghurt and fresh berries, to serve

1. Preheat the oven to 180°C fan, and line a 20cm square baking tin with baking parchment. Measure the oats, seeds, chocolate chips, cocoa powder, ground cinnamon and baking powder into a mixing bowl.
2. Put the milk, eggs, honey and banana into a jug. Whisk well, then pour into the mixing bowl. Stir to combine.
3. Pour into the lined tin and cook for 20 minutes. Leave to cool in the tin for 10 minutes, then cut into slices and serve.

STORAGE:
Store in an airtight container in the fridge for up to 3 days.

TO FREEZE:
Cool the slices completely before freezing. Place them in a labelled ziplock bag and freeze flat. They will keep for up to 3 months.

TO DEFROST:
Take the slices out of the freezer and defrost in an airtight container on the worktop, ready to grab for breakfast.

Prep time. **3 mins**   Cook time. **20 mins**   Cooling time. **10 mins**

Breakfast

It's great to have a recipe that you can make ahead for mornings 'on the go'. If the kids have football matches and dance classes, or you've to grab the bus and eat on the move, breakfast bars can be a lifesaver, along with a very portable banana and a handful of nuts! You can even take these directly from the freezer and put them into a box to take with you, they'll defrost in about an hour.

Blueberry breakfast bars

MAKES 12

FOR THE CRUMBLE BASE & TOPPING
180g plain flour
120g oats
60g brown sugar
½ teaspoon baking powder
90g butter

FOR THE FILLING
230g blueberries (fresh or frozen)
20g caster sugar
½ tablespoon cornflour
juice of ½ a lemon

1. Preheat the oven to 180°C fan and line a 20cm square tin with baking parchment.
2. Measure the flour, oats, brown sugar and baking powder into a bowl, and mix well. Add the butter and work it into the oats and flour with your fingers until it starts to clump together – this will take a few minutes.
3. Tip half the mix into the tin. Push it down and spread it out evenly, making sure to get into the corners. Bake in the oven for 10 minutes. In the meantime mix the blueberries with the caster sugar, cornflour and lemon juice.
4. When the base comes out of the oven, top with the blueberries and scatter over the other half of the crumble mix. Put it back into the oven to bake for another 25–35 minutes.
5. Leave to cool for an hour to set, then cut into bars.

STORAGE:
Store in an airtight container in the fridge for up to 3 days.

TO FREEZE:
The bars should be completely cooled before freezing. Place them in a labelled ziplock bag and freeze flat. They will keep for up to 3 months.

TO DEFROST:
Take the bars out of the freezer and defrost them in an airtight container on the worktop, ready to grab for breakfast.

Prep time. **15 mins**   Cook time. **35 mins**   Cooling time. **1 hour**

I have been making these fritters since my kids were babies. They're sweet, cheesy and easy for any child to hold and feed themselves. I was once invited to do some cooking demos for new parents, and this was one of the recipes I shared that went down really well. They are a great option for breakfast because they are filling and kids can have whatever else they like, such as eggs, ham, and avocado. Once defrosted they are great to reheat in the toaster – add some butter too, if you like.

Sweetcorn & cheese fritters with easy tomato relish

MAKES 12 SMALL FRITTERS

FOR THE FRITTERS

250g tinned sweetcorn, drained
2 eggs
50g grated Cheddar cheese
50–70g self-raising flour (3 heaped tablespoons)
20g butter, melted
olive oil, for cooking

FOR THE RELISH

1 × 400g tin of chopped tomatoes
1 tablespoon tomato purée
1 clove of garlic, peeled and finely grated
2 tablespoons sugar or runny honey
3 tablespoons vinegar, such as malt, white wine or cider
½ teaspoon salt

1. Blend the sweetcorn and eggs together until smooth, or keep them a bit chunky if you prefer. Transfer the mixture to a bowl. Stir in the cheese and flour. The batter should drop off the spoon – if it's too runny add some more flour, if it's too thick add a dash of milk to loosen. Finally, stir in the melted butter.

2. Heat a frying pan on a medium to high heat. Add some oil, then wipe the frying pan with kitchen paper so it's evenly coated (be careful not to burn your fingers). Scoop or spoon the batter into the pan and fry for a few minutes on each side. Transfer to a wire rack, and repeat.

3. Spoon the tomato relish over the fritters and serve with poached eggs and sweet chilli sauce.

FOR THE EASY TOMATO RELISH

Put all the ingredients into a small pan and simmer for 20 minutes on a medium heat until the sauce has reduced and thickened. Keep it chunky, or blend it a little if you prefer.

STORAGE:
This relish keeps in a jar in the fridge for 1 week.

TO FREEZE:
Cool the fritters completely, lay them on a baking tray, freeze flat, then place them in a labelled ziplock bag.

Freeze the relish for up to 3 months.

TO DEFROST:
Defrost the fritters overnight to have for breakfast or add to the lunchbox in the morning.

Defrost the relish in the fridge overnight.

Prep time: **15 mins**   Cook time: **25 mins**

Huevos rancheros means ranch eggs, and this is a super way to serve them at breakfast time! I love adding beans to tomato sauce, and adding Mexican spices makes the dish really tasty. Serve the bean sauce and eggs on soft tortilla wraps. Everyone should be full and happy until lunchtime ... olé!

Huevos rancheros with avocado & sour cream

SERVES 6

- 1 tablespoon cooking oil
- ½ a red pepper, deseeded and sliced
- 2 cloves of garlic, grated or finely chopped
- 1 teaspoon paprika
- 1 teaspoon ground cumin
- ½ teaspoon chilli flakes (optional)
- ½ teaspoon salt
- 1 teaspoon runny honey or sugar
- 1 × 400g tin of chopped tomatoes
- 1 × 400g tin of red kidney beans, drained and rinsed

TO SERVE
- 6 eggs, fried
- 6 small flour tortillas, warmed
- sour cream
- 2 large avocados, sliced
- chopped fresh coriander
- ½ a lime, cut into wedges

1. Warm a wide pot on a medium heat and pour in the cooking oil, followed by the sliced red pepper. Cook for a few minutes to soften. Add the garlic, paprika, cumin, chilli flakes (if using), salt, runny honey and chopped tomatoes. Add a small amount of water to the tin, swirl it around to clean it, and add the water to the pot. Stir the sauce, then simmer for 5 minutes.

2. Add the drained and rinsed kidney beans to the pot and simmer for a further 15 minutes.

3. Put a frying pan on and fry the eggs. Warm the tortilla wraps for a few seconds on a dry warm pan or in the microwave. To serve, add some bean sauce to a warm tortilla, and top with a fried egg, some sour cream, a few slices of avocado, chopped coriander and a squeeze of fresh lime.

STORAGE:
The bean sauce can be cooled and stored in the fridge for up to 3 days.

TO FREEZE:
Cool the bean sauce and store in a labelled freezer bag for up to 3 months.

TO DEFROST:
Defrost in the fridge overnight or in the microwave, using the defrost setting. Reheat in a pan or in the microwave until piping hot.

TIP:
I use tinned tomatoes a lot. They need to be cooked for at least 20 minutes for the metallic taste to disappear and for the flavours to mingle in the sauce.

 Prep time. **20 mins**   Cook time. **30 mins**

Breakfast

I recently learned that long ago the English called eggy bread 'Gypsy bread'. It was peasant food for those who couldn't afford meat. It's just like French toast or eggy bread and it's a genius way to get eggs into kids in the morning! It works best with old or stale bread, which is a great way to avoid food waste and serve up something delicious.

Gypsy bread with mixed berry compote

SERVES 2

FOR THE GYPSY BREAD
2 eggs
100ml milk
½ teaspoon ground cinnamon
olive oil and butter, for cooking
4 thick slices of bread
  (see miracle loaf, page 194)

FOR THE BERRY COMPOTE
350g mixed fresh or frozen berries
  (raspberries, blackcurrants,
  blackberries, etc.)
2 tablespoons sugar or honey
  (add more if needed)
juice of ¼ of a lemon

TO SERVE
yoghurt
runny nut butter

FOR THE BERRY COMPOTE

1. Put the berries into a small pot and warm them over a low heat until completely heated through (there's no need to add water).

2. Add the sugar and simmer for 2–3 minutes.

3. Mash the fruit to break up the bigger berries. Stir through the lemon juice. Taste and adjust the sweetness or sourness if needed. Set aside to cool.

FOR THE GYPSY BREAD

1. Warm a large non-stick frying pan on a medium heat. Crack the eggs into a shallow bowl, pour in the milk and cinnamon, and whisk well. Spray the pan with oil. Dip the bread into the egg mix and coat both sides, shaking off any excess. Lay the first slice in the pan, then repeat with the second slice.

2. Cook for 1–2 minutes, then flip and cook the other side. Serve straight away with the compote and sides. Repeat with the other slices.

STORAGE:
Once cooled, the compote will keep in an airtight container in the fridge for up to 5 days.

TO FREEZE:
Freeze the compote in an airtight container or labelled ziplock bag for up to 3 months. The finished Gypsy bread isn't suitable for freezing.

TO DEFROST:
Defrost the compote in the fridge overnight, or at room temperature for 2 hours.

TIP:
When possible, I like to use home-made bread for this recipe. Thick slices of my Miracle loaf are ideal. Otherwise, use whatever bread you have to hand. If the bread is a day or two old, that works even better.

To get ahead, have portioned slices of miracle bread and small pots of compote ready to grab from the freezer. Defrost overnight for breakfast next morning.

 Prep time. **15 mins** Cook time. **25 mins**

Breakfast

My daughter asked for a waffle-maker for her seventh birthday. We bought an inexpensive one, not thinking it would get much use, but in fact we have used it so much, and learned to make lots of tasty savoury waffles on it too. Top waffle-maker tips: heat it well and grease it well. If it's not hot enough or greased enough the waffles will stick.

This recipe is perfect for leftover mashed potatoes. YUM.

Cheesy potato waffles

MAKES 10

500g mashed potato (made with butter and salt)
130g plain flour
100g Cheddar cheese, grated
2 eggs, beaten
cooking oil, to grease

1. Preheat the waffle-maker and grease it. I use cooking oil and a piece of kitchen paper to coat it well. If you don't have a waffle-maker, you can cook these waffles like pancakes in a frying pan.
2. Put the mashed potato into a large mixing bowl, then add the flour and cheese and mix well. Add salt and pepper to taste. Pour in the beaten eggs and mix to form a dough, using your hands. Divide into 10 equal pieces and roll them into balls.
3. If you have a 2-piece waffle-maker, cook 2 at a time. Make sure the waffle-maker is nice and hot – they vary, but it's important to cook the waffles until they are brown and crispy on the outside, which will take 4–5 minutes usually. Remove and place on a wire rack while you cook the rest.
4. Serve warm, with eggs and beans.

STORAGE:
The waffles will keep for up to 3 days in the fridge.

TO FREEZE:
Freeze the waffles flat on a tray, then place in a labelled ziplock bag in the freezer. They are good for up to 3 months.

TO DEFROST:
Leave in the fridge overnight, ready for an easy breakfast in the morning. Reheat in the air fryer for 4 minutes at 180°C or in the oven for 10 minutes at 180°C fan.

TIP:
To avoid wet mash it's best to steam the potatoes if possible. If you boil them, make sure to drain them well, return them to the hot pan and let them dry out a bit, then mash with butter and salt.

Image on page 39

Prep time. **10 mins**   Cook time. **20 mins**

Breakfast

Some days I'm more organized than others, and on the days I'm super on it, I love to make these easy muffins. They are so easy and tasty, and I love an individually portioned piece. They are portable and can be eaten hot or cold. Great for breakfast, or they can be popped into the lunchbox – just make sure it's chilled in a cool-bag until lunchtime. This works really well with leftover sausages from the night before.

Sausage & egg muffin cups

MAKES 12

8 eggs
3 tablespoons cottage cheese
4 sausages
4 cherry tomatoes, chopped
80g Cheddar cheese, grated

1. Cook the sausages in the oven or air fryer until golden brown and cooked through, then cool and slice.
2. Preheat the oven to 180°C fan and lightly oil a 12-hole muffin tin.
3. Whisk the eggs in a mixing bowl. Stir in the cottage cheese and a small pinch of salt and pepper.
4. Divide the sliced sausages between the 12 holes in the tin, top with the egg mixture, add the chopped cherry tomatoes, and finish with grated Cheddar.
5. Bake for about 20 minutes, then take them from the oven and allow to cool. Once cooled, use a knife to free the egg muffins from the tin.

STORAGE:
Once cooled, store in an airtight container in the fridge for up to 3 days.

TO FREEZE:
Place the muffins flat in labelled ziplock bags and freeze for up to 3 months.

TO DEFROST:
Defrost in an airtight container in the fridge overnight. Eat cold the next day, or reheat in the oven or the microwave until heated through to the centre.

Image on page 38

Prep time. **15 mins**   Cook time. **20 mins**

Chapter 2

Savoury Lunchboxes

These are always a hit in our house, the perfect portable sausage in a pastry casing. I couldn't help sneaking in some goodness here with the carrot and oats. If you're feeling adventurous, try adding grated apple and chopped sage as well, or some honey and wholegrain mustard. Ideal for the lunchbox, for a picnic or a party, these can be enjoyed hot or cold.

Mini sausage rolls

MAKES 16

- 400g sausage meat or sausages, casings removed
- 1 medium carrot, grated (70g)
- 1 teaspoon ground cumin
- 1 teaspoon paprika
- 15g oats
- 1 × 375g pack of ready-rolled puff pastry
- 1 egg, beaten, to glaze
- 1 tablespoon sesame seeds (optional)

1. Preheat the oven to 180°C fan and line a baking tray with baking parchment.
2. Put the sausage meat, grated carrot, cumin, paprika and oats into a bowl and mix well.
3. Unroll the puff pastry and cut it in half lengthways.
4. Divide the sausage mixture into two equal pieces and spread one along the length of each pastry strip in an even sausage shape, leaving a 1cm edge.
5. Brush the edges with egg, then tightly wrap the pastry around the sausage meat. Gently press a fork all along the seam to help it seal well.
6. Cut each roll into 8 pieces with a sharp knife and arrange on a baking sheet.
7. Brush with beaten egg, sprinkle with sesame seeds (if using), and bake in the oven for 30 minutes until golden brown and cooked through.

STORAGE:
Store the rolls in an airtight container in the fridge for up to 3 days.

TO FREEZE:
Freeze raw or cooked. Freeze the rolls in labelled ziplock bags for up to 3 months. To cook the raw sausage rolls from frozen, place them on a baking tray and follow step 7 and add 5 extra minutes.

TO DEFROST:
Defrost in the fridge overnight.

TIP:
I like to take the pastry out of the fridge 30 minutes before I use it, so that it softens and is easier to work with.

These sausage rolls are tasty hot or cold. To reheat them, put them into a preheated oven at 180°C fan or an air fryer at 180°C for 10–15 minutes, or until piping hot.

Prep time. **20 mins**   Cook time. **30 mins**

These mini pies remind me of my time in New Zealand – every corner shop had a hot-hold selling pies, and bacon and cheese was my favourite! I love a kitchen cheat, and buying pre-made pastry is one of them. Once the pie cases are baked, the rest is easy. My daughter just loves these in her lunchbox.

Mini bacon & cheese quiches

MAKES 12

150g chopped bacon
1 × 320g pack of ready-rolled shortcrust pastry
plain flour, for dusting

2 medium eggs
140ml cream
a pinch of salt
80g Cheddar cheese, grated

1. Preheat the oven to 180°C fan.
2. Grease a 12-hole metal muffin tin and dust with flour, then turn the tray upside down over the sink and knock out the excess. Unroll the pastry, then using a large cookie cutter or glass, cut out 12 discs a bit larger than the muffin tin hole, rolling the offcuts of pastry if needed. Place a paper muffin case on each pastry disc and press down. Then fill with baking beans or dry uncooked rice. Bake in the oven for 15 minutes, then carefully remove the paper cases and beans and bake for another 3–5 minutes. Set the quiche cases aside to cool.
3. While the pastry bakes, fry the bacon in a frying pan until crispy, then remove and place on kitchen paper to take off the extra grease. Crack the eggs into a mixing bowl along with the cream and pinch of salt, and whisk well.
4. Divide the bacon and cheese into each of the 12 pastry cases. Pour over the cream and egg mixture. Carefully put the tray into the oven and bake for 20 minutes, until set.

STORAGE:
Store the quiches in an airtight container in the fridge for up to 3 days.

TO FREEZE:
Freeze in labelled ziplock bags for up to 3 months.

TO DEFROST:
Defrost in the fridge overnight.

TIP:
To make these meat-free, swap the bacon for some roasted red peppers, or sweetcorn or peas.

 Prep time. **20 mins**   Cook time. **40 mins**

Homemade oatcakes are on a different level to the ones you buy in the shops – they are so good. They are great for lunchboxes and as a snack plate with chopped fruit and veg sticks too.

I like to serve them after school with grapes, apple, cheese, apricot jam and mixed nuts. They also make a well-balanced lunch with homemade butterbean hummus and carrot sticks.

Oatcakes with butterbean hummus

MAKES APPROX 12.

FOR THE OATCAKES
- 200g rolled oats
- 50g plain flour, plus extra for dusting
- 1 tsp salt
- ½ tsp sugar
- ½ tsp bicarbonate of soda
- 50g butter
- 70–80ml boiling water

FOR THE BUTTERBEAN HUMMUS
- 1 × 400g tin of butterbeans, drained
- 1 clove of garlic, peeled and finely chopped
- ½ a lemon, zest and juice
- 1 teaspoon ground cumin
- 2 tablespoons light tahini
- salt, to taste
- 60ml boiled water
- 2 tablespoons olive oil

1. Preheat the oven to 170°C fan and line a large baking tray with baking parchment. Put the oats, flour, salt, sugar and bicarbonate of soda into a mixing bowl. Then, using your fingers, rub the butter into the flour mix until it looks like coarse sand.
2. Little by little pour in the boiling water until the dough comes together – if it's dry, add more water, if it's wet, add more flour. Dust the worktop and roll out the dough to about ½cm thick, then cut out circles with a 5cm cookie cutter; the number you get will depend on the size of your cutter.
3. Place on the baking tray and bake in the oven for 20 minutes. Cool completely.

FOR THE BUTTERBEAN HUMMUS

Put everything into a small powerful blender and blend to your desired consistency – keep it chunky or blend until really smooth. Taste and adjust with more salt or lemon, and if it's too thick add more water.

STORAGE:
The oatcakes will keep in an airtight container for up to a week.

Keep the hummus in an airtight container in the fridge for up to 5 days.

TO FREEZE:
Freeze the oatcakes in a labelled ziplock bag for up to 3 months.

Freeze the hummus in an airtight container for up to 3 months.

TO DEFROST:
Defrost the oatcakes in an airtight container on the worktop for an hour, or overnight

Defrost the hummus in the fridge overnight, ready to use the next day for lunch.

Prep time. 20 mins   Cook time. 20 mins

Savoury Lunchboxes

There are certain foods that kids seem to enjoy without fuss, and pesto is one of them. It's a great way to add flavour and green goodness. You can absolutely make your own, but there are some great fresh pestos in the shops too. I love to bake these scrolls on Sunday evenings, as they only take 10 minutes or so to make. They make great finger food for parties too – just remember to put your spare hand under your chin to catch the flaky crumbs!

Pesto & cheese pastry scrolls

MAKES 12

1 × 375g pack of ready-rolled puff pastry
60g cream cheese
60g green pesto
60g carrots, grated
60g Cheddar cheese, grated

1. Preheat the oven to 180°C fan and line a large baking tray with baking parchment.
2. Unroll the puff pastry. Using a butter knife, spread an even layer of the cream cheese all over the pastry. Top with an even layer of pesto, followed by the grated carrot and Cheddar cheese.
3. Starting at the long edge, roll the pastry carefully into a log. Using a fork, gently press down and seal the pastry along the seam.
4. Cut the log into 12 equal pieces. Place them flat on the baking tray and bake for 25–30 minutes, until golden and cooked through.
5. These can be eaten warm or cold.

 STORAGE:
Once cooled, these will keep in the fridge in an airtight container for up to 3 days.

 TO FREEZE:
Freeze flat on a tray, then transfer to labelled ziplock bags, freeze for up to 3 months.

 TO DEFROST:
Defrost in the fridge overnight and pop into lunchboxes in the morning.

 TIP:
Leave the pastry out of the fridge for 20 minutes to warm up before using, so it's easier to work with.

Image on page 50–51

 Prep time. **15 mins**   Cook time. **25–30 mins**

I am never without a bag of garden peas in the freezer – in fact, I'd say I overstock with frozen peas!! Of all the frozen veggies they are my favourite, for a quick dinner, a fast pea pesto or for these tasty pancakes. My kids aren't so keen on feta, they find it dry and salty, so you can swap it for Cheddar if you like. These flavours remind me of a great holiday I had in Crete – the food there was vibrant and simple. The mint adds great freshness and goes perfectly with the peas.

Pea, mint & feta pancakes

MAKES 8

75g self-raising flour
100ml milk
2 eggs
150g frozen peas, thawed

100g feta, crumbled, or grated Cheddar
1 tbsp chopped fresh mint leaves
a small pinch of salt and pepper
oil, for cooking

1. Sieve the flour into a bowl. Measure the milk into a jug, crack in the eggs and whisk well, then pour into the bowl of flour and stir to make a batter.

2. Mash the peas almost to a paste, then add them to the bowl along with the crumbled feta, chopped mint and salt and pepper.

3. Warm a large frying pan and lightly coat with oil. Spoon on 2 tablespoons of the mix per pancake. Wait for the bubbles to appear – it will take a few minutes – then flip and cook for another minute. Transfer to a wire rack to cool.

4. Eat warm or cold.

STORAGE:
The pancakes will keep in the fridge for up to 3 days.

TO FREEZE:
Freeze flat on a tray. Once frozen, place in labelled ziplock bags for up to 3 months.

TO DEFROST:
Defrost in the fridge overnight, and reheat in the microwave for a couple of seconds or in the toaster until heated through.

Image on page 50–51

Prep time. 10 mins   Cook time. 15 mins

Savoury scones are so delicious and are often overlooked. This is a hybrid scone with all the flavours of pizza! You can go for a plain margarita, ham and cheese, or even add pineapple for a Hawaiian. We like them with butter in the lunchbox, but feel free to add salad and extra ham or cheese.

Pizza scones

MAKES 8

140ml milk, approx. (depending on the mix – you may need more or less!)
2 eggs
2 tablespoons pesto rosso (red pesto)
400g plain flour
2½ teaspoons baking powder
100g salted butter, at room temperature
100g Cheddar and mozzarella cheese, grated
50g mild pepperoni or ham, diced

TOPPING (OPTIONAL)
2 tablespoons pesto rosso
50g Cheddar and mozzarella cheese, grated
50g ham or pepperoni

1. Preheat the oven to 180°C fan. Line a baking tray with baking parchment. Put the milk, eggs and pesto rosso into a jug, and whisk well with a fork. Sieve the flour and baking powder into a mixing bowl, and stir to combine.

2. Rub the butter into the flour with your fingertips until there are no big lumps. Stir in the cheese and pepperoni.

3. Pour in the milky red egg mix bit by bit (you may not need it all). Bring the dough together with a fork. If it still seems dry, add bit more milk. Tip the dough on to a floured worktop and gently knead until it's smooth. Be very gentle, don't overwork it.

4. Put the dough on the lined tray and push to flatten into a round. Flour a large knife to stop the dough sticking, then cut the dough into 8 wedges, like a pizza. Separate each wedge, leaving space for them to rise. If using the toppings, spread a layer of pesto rosso on the top of each one, then some cheese and a small slice of pepperoni. Bake for 20–22 minutes.

5. These scones are delicious warm and fresh. If eating cold, slice in half and add butter.

STORAGE:
Once cooled, keep in an airtight container in the fridge for up to 3 days.

TO FREEZE:
Freeze in labelled ziplock bags for up to 3 months.

TO DEFROST:
Defrost in the fridge overnight.

Prep time. **15 mins**   Cook time. **20–22 mins**

Hand pies are just filled pastries you can hold in your hand. They are flaky and just delicious. I'm a huge fan of salty-and-sweet savoury food. Salty goat's cheese and sweet potato are a fabulous combination with the addition of the mildly spiced onions.

Sweet potato & goat's cheese hand pies

MAKES 6

1½ tablespoons oil
1 medium onion, finely diced
2 cloves of garlic, finely chopped
1 teaspoon ground cumin
1 teaspoon paprika
a small pinch of salt and pepper

100g sweet potato cubes, cooked
100g goat's cheese
1 × 375g pack of ready-rolled puff pastry
1 egg, beaten with a dash of milk to make egg wash

1. Warm a frying pan on a medium heat, then add the oil and onion and cook for 5–10 minutes, until soft. Add the garlic, cumin, paprika and salt and pepper, and cook for a further few minutes. Transfer to a plate to cool.

2. Preheat the oven to 180°C fan. Line a large baking tray with baking parchment. Put the cooked sweet potatoes into a mixing bowl with the goat's cheese and cooked onions and mix, but leave small lumps of cheese and sweet potato – it's better if it's not a smooth paste.

3. Unroll the pastry and cut it into 6 equal squares. Brush the edge of each square with the egg wash. Add a generous tablespoon of the filling to each square, then fold the pastry over to make a triangle, sealing the edge with a fork. Brush the pies with the egg wash.

4. Bake in the oven for 30 minutes, until golden and cooked through.

STORAGE:
The pies can be kept in the fridge for up to 3 days.

TO FREEZE:
Freeze in labelled ziplock bags for up to 3 months.

TO DEFROST:
Defrost in the fridge over-night.

TIP:
You can make these with puff or shortcrust pastry.

I like to peel, dice, steam and freeze sweet potatoes so as to have them on hand for this recipe and for my sweet potato pancakes on page 220.

Prep time. 20 mins   Cook time. 30 mins

These simple fritters are so tasty and pack in some real goodness. When I was weaning my daughter I liked to give her different tastes and textures, so cooked vegetable fritters were always popular. I would cut them into strips so she could feed herself. As she got older I added some spices and she still loves them for her lunch.

Sweet potato & carrot fritters

MAKES 12

2 carrots (200g)
1 medium sweet potato (250g)
2 teaspoons mild curry powder
salt and pepper, to taste
100g self-raising flour
oil, for cooking

1. Grate the carrots and sweet potato into a mixing bowl. Spoon in the curry powder, salt and pepper, and stir well.
2. Sprinkle the flour all over the grated veggies and use your hands to mix really well – this will take a few minutes. Give the mix a really good squeeze and mix it like a dough. The liquid from the veg will help to form a batter with the flour.
3. Warm a frying pan on a medium heat, and add two tablespoons of oil. Shape the mix into small fritters using two spoons and fry for a couple of minutes, then flip and fry again until cooked through. Transfer to a wire rack and repeat.
4. The fritters can be eaten hot or cold.

STORAGE:
Once cooled, the fritters will keep in the fridge in an airtight container for up to 3 days.

TO FREEZE:
Freeze flat on a tray, then transfer to labelled ziplock bags for up to 3 months.

TO DEFROST:
Defrost in the fridge overnight and pop into the lunchbox in the morning.

Prep time. **10 mins**   Cook time. **20 mins**

I could write a whole cookbook on muffins … and maybe I will one day. Sweet and savoury muffins are always a winner at lunchtime. These ones are delicious when warm and fresh, but when they cool it's best to cut them in half and add some butter. These are ideal with soup on a winter's day or with cheese slices and pickles on a sunny afternoon.

Courgette & sweetcorn muffins

MAKES 12

1 courgette (150g)
225g self-raising flour
75g tinned sweetcorn, drained
100g Cheddar cheese, grated
salt and pepper, to taste
175ml milk
50ml olive oil
1 egg

1. Preheat the oven to 170°C fan, and line a muffin tin with paper cases. Grate the courgette, then put it into a sieve and squeeze out the extra moisture.
2. Measure the flour, sweetcorn and Cheddar cheese into a mixing bowl, then add the grated courgette and a pinch of salt and pepper, and stir together.
3. In a jug, whisk together the milk, oil and egg, and pour into the mixing bowl. Stir to combine, then spoon the mixture into the paper cases. Bake for 18 minutes, or until golden and cooked through.

STORAGE:
The muffins will keep in the fridge for up to 3 days.

TO FREEZE:
Freeze in labelled ziplock bags for up to 3 months.

TO DEFROST:
Defrost in the fridge overnight.

Prep time. **15 mins**   Cook time. **20 mins**

I've been making frittatas for years. It's such a clever dish to cook and fill with nutritious ingredients. I've kept this one pretty simple, but you could add leftover potatoes, carrots, peas or pretty much anything you fancy. Salmon is a great source of omega-3 vitamins and healthy fats – as I tell my kids, it's brain food to help them get smarter than me!

Salmon & broccoli frittata slices

MAKES 6

2 fillets of salmon (240g)
4 broccoli florets (100g)
6 eggs

50g Cheddar cheese, grated, plus 20g for the top

1. Put a small pan of water on to boil, then reduce to a simmer, add the salmon fillets and cook for 8–10 minutes. Place on a plate to cool, then flake into bite-size pieces.
2. In a separate small pan, boil the broccoli florets until tender, then drain, cool and chop into bite-size pieces.
3. Preheat the oven to 180°C fan and grease a 20cm baking tin really well. Crack the eggs into a mixing bowl and beat with a fork. Mix in the Cheddar cheese and the chopped broccoli and flaked salmon. Pour into the prepared tin and top with the extra cheese.
4. Bake for 20–25 minutes, until just set and golden on top. Leave to cool for 5 minutes, then slice and remove from the tin using a spatula.
5. These can be eaten hot or cold.

STORAGE:
Store in an airtight container for up to 3 days.

TO FREEZE:
Place the slices in labelled ziplock bags and freeze for up to 3 months.

TO DEFROST:
Defrost in the fridge overnight. If reheating, place in a preheated oven at 180°C fan or an air fryer at 180°C for 10 minutes, until heated through.

Prep time. **20 mins**   Cook time. **20–25 mins**

Chapter 3

Sweet Lunchboxes

Sweet Lunchboxes

There are some recipes in this book that were stepping-stones to get to where I am today! In November 2023 I shared a montage reel of me making snacks for the lunchbox. That reel was a viral hit and brought me a huge number of new followers. These energy balls played a starring role, and they have been made for thousands of kids' lunchboxes across the world! So cool to see.

Nut-free energy balls

MAKES 12

115g pitted dates
40g rolled oats
60g mixed seeds
20g desiccated coconut, plus 20g extra to finish
1 tablespoon cocoa powder

1. Put the dates into a bowl, cover with boiling water, leave to soften for 10 minutes. Meanwhile, blend the oats, seeds, coconut and cocoa powder in a processor – the texture should be coarse and not too fine.
2. Drain the dates and add them to the blender, then blend until it looks like a thick paste. If it looks dry and won't clump, add a dash of boiled water and blend again.
3. Roll the mixture into balls, big or small – whichever you prefer.
4. To finish, pour the extra desiccated coconut into a wide bowl. Lightly wet your hands to help the coconut stick, then roll the balls again and toss them in the coconut. Put the balls into a container and pop them into the fridge to firm up.

STORAGE:
Keep these in the fridge for up to 7 days.

TO FREEZE:
Freeze in a labelled ziplock bag for up to 3 months.

TO DEFROST:
Defrost in an airtight container on the worktop overnight.

TIP:
To change up the flavour, add ½ teaspoon of orange zest to the blended mix.

Image on page 64

Prep time. **20 mins**

I never saw myself as a baker. When I trained as a chef I was drawn to the larder, the savoury side of the kitchen. But now, as a mum, I much prefer to bake, and scones are one of my all-time favourites. My mini scones are always popular when I share them on my social pages. Cheap, quick, and easy to make and freeze.

Mini sweet scones

MAKES 16 MINI OR 8 LARGE

150ml milk, approx.
2 eggs
400g self-raising flour, plus extra for dusting
100g butter, at room temperature, cut into cubes
2 tablespoons sugar
1 egg and a dash of milk, beaten, to make egg wash

1. Preheat the oven to 180°C fan and line a large baking tray with baking parchment.
2. Measure the milk into a jug, crack in the eggs and mix well, then set to one side. Measure the flour into a large mixing bowl, and add the butter and the sugar. Rub the butter into the flour and sugar, using your fingers, until it resembles breadcrumbs.
3. Make a well in the middle of the flour and pour in the milk and egg mix. Stir in with a fork, then tip the dough on to a floured worktop and use your hands to gently knead it into a smooth round. If the dough is dry, add a bit more milk, if it's sticky, add more flour. Flatten the dough out to a thickness of 1.5 inches.
4. Dip the mini cutter into the bag of flour and tap off the extra flour – this stops the scones sticking to the cutter. Cut out the scones, putting them on the lined tray. Repeat until all the dough is used up. Brush the scones with egg wash.
5. Bake for 18 minutes, until golden and light when lifted. Place on a rack to cool completely.

 STORAGE:
Store the scones in an airtight container for up to 3 days.

 TO FREEZE:
Freeze in labelled ziplock bags for up to 3 months.

 TO DEFROST:
Defrost in an airtight container on the worktop overnight.

 TIP:
I use a 5cm mini cookie cutter to make these scones.

Image on page 65

 Prep time. **15 mins**   Cook time. **20 mins**

Oaty squares of crunchy, crumbly goodness – who doesn't love a flapjack? Most flapjacks are sugar-dense, but these are definitely a healthier version. If I could take one ingredient with me to a desert island it would be oats – they are so versatile and nutritious, and I love the oaty flavour. I've kept these nut-free so they are suitable for the school lunchbox.

Seed & date flapjacks

MAKES 12

8 pitted dates, chopped
180g oats
½ teaspoon ground cinnamon
40g mixed seeds, such as pumpkin/sunflower
75g honey
100g coconut oil, melted

1. Preheat the oven to 180°C fan and line a 20cm baking tin with baking parchment. Put the dates into a bowl, cover with boiling water, leave to soften for 10 minutes, then drain and discard the water.

2. Measure the oats, cinnamon and mixed seeds into a mixing bowl, then add the chopped dates and give it all a stir. Melt the coconut oil in the microwave or a small pan and stir in the honey. Pour the wet mixture into the dry ingredients and mix well until everything is combined.

3. Transfer to the prepared baking tin and press it down firmly, using a square of baking parchment to push down with your hands. Bake for about 20–25 minutes, or until the flapjacks are golden brown.

4. Remove from the oven and let the flapjacks cool in the pan for about 10 minutes, then place them on a wire rack to cool completely. Cut into squares.

STORAGE:
Store the flapjacks in an airtight container for up to a week.

TO FREEZE:
Freeze in labelled ziplock bags for up to 3 months.

TO DEFROST:
Defrost in an airtight container on the worktop overnight.

Prep time. **15 mins**   Cook time. **25 mins**   Cooling time. **10 mins**

I first baked these for my online kids' cooking classes back in 2021. I remember adding a drizzle of chocolate to the first batch to photograph and help me promote my class – that one was a sellout! Some of the best recipes are the simple ones. These are great to make with your kids – let them decide what flavours they want to add so they can make them their own.

Easy oat bars

MAKES 12

180g oats
60g brown sugar
½ teaspoon ground cinnamon
1 banana, mashed, or 1 apple, peeled and grated
100ml milk

2 eggs
1 teaspoon vanilla extract
Optional add-ins: seeds, raisins, cranberries, desiccated coconut, chocolate chips, orange zest, lime zest, chopped nuts

1. Preheat the oven to 180°C fan. Grease and line a 20cm square baking tray or similar.
2. Mix everything together in a mixing bowl. Transfer to the baking tray and smooth the mix with the back of a fork. Bake for 25–30 minutes, until golden brown.
3. Cool, then slice into bars.

STORAGE:
These bars keep in an airtight container for up to 3 days.

TO FREEZE:
Freeze in labelled ziplock bags for up to 3 months.

TO DEFROST:
Defrost in the lunchbox the night before you need them.

Image on page 68

Prep time. **10 mins**   Cook time. **30 mins**

My cousins and I used to pinch raspberries from my neighbour's garden when we were small. I know it was naughty, but they were just so plump and sharp, sweet and irresistible! I can still taste them now. Raspberries are my favourite fruit, and they are so good in these special crumble muffins. I prefer to use frozen raspberries – they hold well in the batter, so that you have bursts of fruit when you bite into your muffin.

Raspberry & ricotta muffins with crumble topping

MAKES 12

FOR THE CRUMBLE TOPPING
50g plain flour
20g soft brown sugar
35g soft butter

FOR THE MUFFINS
250g self-raising flour
1 teaspoon bicarbonate of soda
90g caster sugar
zest of 1 lemon
125g frozen raspberries
180g ricotta
100ml vegetable oil
2 eggs
2 tablespoons lemon juice

1. Preheat the oven to 180°C fan and line a 12-hole muffin tin with paper cases.
2. Put all the crumble ingredients into a bowl and rub together with your fingers until the mix resembles wet sand. Set aside. Sift the self-raising flour and bicarbonate of soda into a mixing bowl, add the sugar and lemon zest, and stir well with a spoon. Make sure the bicarbonate of soda is well combined. Tip in the raspberries and gently mix them through the flour.
3. Put the ricotta, vegetable oil, eggs and lemon juice into a jug and whisk well with a fork. Add the ricotta mix to the flour mix and gently stir in with a wooden spoon or a rubber spatula. Gently fold the mix until no flour remains visible.
4. Using an ice cream scoop or a dessertspoon, divide the batter evenly between the muffin cases. Sprinkle the crumble over the top. Bake for 20–25 minutes. To check they are cooked, pierce one with a cocktail stick – when it comes out clean, they are ready.

STORAGE:
Store the muffins in an airtight container for up to 3 days.

TO FREEZE:
Freeze in labelled ziplock bags for up to 3 months.

TO DEFROST:
Defrost in an airtight container on the worktop overnight.

Prep time. 15 mins   Cook time. 20–25 mins

If you're going to send a cookie to school it's probably best that it nourishes the school-goer and helps them to concentrate. I remember being sluggish in the afternoons at school. Those last couple of hours can be tough going, so milk and a school cookie to the rescue.

School cookies

MAKES APPROX. 16

100g rolled oats
50g sunflower seeds
75g raisins
100g wholemeal flour
1 tsp baking powder

25g desiccated coconut
zest of ½ an orange
100g butter, softened
100g soft light brown sugar
1 egg

1. Preheat the oven to 170°C fan and line two baking trays with baking parchment. Blend the oats, sunflower seeds and raisins together, until they have a coarse texture. Transfer into a mixing bowl, add the wholemeal flour, baking powder, coconut and orange zest, and mix well.

2. In a separate bowl, blend the softened butter and sugar until pale and fluffy, then beat in the egg. Fold through the dry ingredients and mix to form a dough. Then divide into 16 even balls, using a spoon or an ice cream scoop. Place on the prepared trays and push each one down with the palm of your hand.

3. Bake for about 15–18 minutes. Leave to cool, then transfer to a wire rack.

 STORAGE:
These are soft cookies. Store them in an airtight container for up to 2 days.

 TO FREEZE:
Freeze in labelled ziplock bags for up to 3 months.

 TO DEFROST:
Defrost in an airtight container on the worktop overnight.

 TIP:
Feel free to add a few chocolate chips just before baking.

Image on page 74

Prep time. **15 mins**   Cook time. **18 mins**

Not just for small kids, big kids love them too. As a parent, you'll always feel better giving your kids homemade snacks. Knowing there's lots of wholesome ingredients added makes that feeling extra-special. These are the best for those mumma/dad little wins!

ABC muffins (apple/banana/carrot)

MAKES 12 REGULAR

200g self-raising flour
50g oats, plus extra for the tops
80g caster sugar
1 teaspoon ground cinnamon
1 teaspoon baking powder
1 medium apple, grated
1 carrot, grated
1 banana, mashed
100g butter, melted
100ml milk
2 eggs

1. Preheat the oven to 180°C fan and line a 12-hole muffin tin with paper cases.
2. Measure the flour, oats, sugar, cinnamon and baking powder into a large bowl, and mix well. Add the apple, carrot and banana to the bowl and mix with a fork.
3. Put the melted butter, milk and eggs into a jug and whisk well.
4. Pour the wet ingredients into the bowl and stir to combine. Scoop the mixture into the muffin tins, sprinkle oats on top and bake in the oven for 20–25 minutes, until golden on top and cooked through. Test them with a cocktail stick – when it comes out clean, they're done.

STORAGE:
Store the muffins in an airtight container for up to 5 days.

TO FREEZE:
Freeze in labelled ziplock bags for up to 3 months.

TO DEFROST:
Defrost in an airtight container on the worktop overnight.

Image on page 75

Prep time. **15 mins**   Cook time. **25 mins**

If you want to cook with seasonal fruit in Ireland or the UK, then apples are an all-year-rounder. I love to bake with apples – once baked they are soft and sweet, and there's something very homely about an apple cake. Yes, you can pack some off in the lunchbox, but enjoy your own slice with a nice mug of tea.

Apple & raisin slice

MAKES 12

- 50g raisins
- 110g plain flour
- 115g wholewheat flour
- 100g soft light brown sugar
- 2 teaspoons baking powder
- 1 teaspoon ground cinnamon
- ½ teaspoon mixed spice
- 3 large apples, peeled and diced
- 150g light-flavoured oil (olive/sunflower/vegetable)
- 3 eggs
- 2 tablespoons oats, for topping

1. Soak the raisins in boiling water for 30 minutes, then drain.
2. Preheat the oven to 170°C fan and line a 20cm square baking tin with baking parchment.
3. Weigh the flours, sugar, baking powder, cinnamon and mixed spice into a large bowl, and mix well. Stir through the diced apple and the drained raisins.
4. Measure the oil into a jug, crack in the eggs and whisk. Add the wet mix to the bowl and stir to combine. Pour the mixture into the prepared baking tin and sprinkle the oats on top.
5. Bake in the oven for 30–40 minutes. To check that the cake is cooked, insert a cocktail stick – when it comes out clean, it's ready. Set aside to cool.

 STORAGE:
Store the cake in an airtight container for up to 3 days.

 TO FREEZE:
Freeze in a labelled ziplock bag for up to 3 months.

 TO DEFROST:
Defrost in an airtight container on the worktop overnight.

Prep time. **25 mins plus soaking** Cook time. **40 mins**

These are a tropical treat, with a great texture and a zingy flavour. I've been making energy balls for years and using different types of dried fruit can really change up the flavours. Apricot and coconut go really well together. Apricots are a rich source of fibre and vitamin A, which is great for our immune system. These also have oats for slow-release energy and chia seeds for protein, making them a great little power snack for the lunchbox.

Apricot & coconut bliss balls

MAKES 12

70g oats
20g desiccated coconut
1 tablespoon chia seeds
200g dried apricots, diced

2 tablespoons coconut oil, melted
2 tablespoons maple syrup
 or honey

1. Place the oats, coconut and chia seeds in a food processor and pulse briefly.
2. Add the diced apricots, coconut oil and maple syrup or honey, and blend until combined. Test the mix – if it's a little dry, add more maple syrup.
3. Roll into balls and place in the fridge for 1 hour.

 STORAGE:
Store these in an airtight container for up to 7 days.

 TO FREEZE:
Freeze in labelled ziplock bags for up to 3 months.

 TO DEFROST:
Defrost in an airtight container on the worktop overnight.

Image on page 80

 Prep time. **15 mins plus chilling**

When I came up with the idea for these, I was thinking lemon drizzle cake. But of course the drizzle cake needs that sugary topping, and I'm always trying to reduce the sugar. I thought blueberries might compensate for the drizzle, and I think I pulled it off! These are sweet, tart and perfectly dinky for the lunchbox.

Lemon & blueberry mini loaves

MAKES 12

200g self-raising flour
80g caster sugar
zest of 1 lemon
80g frozen blueberries

100ml vegetable oil
150ml milk
1 egg
2 tablespoons lemon juice

1. Preheat the oven to 170°C fan and put a mini silicone loaf mould on a baking tray.
2. Sieve the flour and caster sugar into a mixing bowl. Add the lemon zest and mix to combine. Tumble in the blueberries and stir to coat in the flour.
3. Whisk the vegetable oil, milk, egg and lemon juice together in a jug, then pour this into the mixing bowl.
4. Gently combine the mixture and spoon evenly into the moulds, making sure each contains at least a couple of blueberries.
5. Bake for 20 minutes, then check they are cooked by inserting a cocktail stick – when it comes out clean the mini loaves are done. After a few minutes, take them out of the moulds and transfer them to a wire rack to cool completely.

STORAGE:
Store these in an airtight container for up to 3 days.

TO FREEZE:
Freeze in labelled ziplock bags for up to 3 months.

TO DEFROST:
Defrost in an airtight container on the worktop overnight.

TIP:
Keep a stash of frozen blueberries in the freezer. They are delicious in baked slices and cakes, little pops of goodness.

Image on page 81

Prep time. 10 mins   Cook time. 20 mins

Chapter 4

Soups & Smoothies

Big bowls of soup are so nourishing and comforting and I am lucky to say my kids love soup. This soup is really handy because all of the ingredients are just roasted together either in the oven or air fryer and then blended with hot stock! Roasting vegetables brings out the sweetness and gives this soup a great depth of flavour. My kids love this in their thermos with a slice of buttered bread for dipping.

Roast tomato & red pepper soup

SERVES 4

- 800g ripe tomatoes, cut into quarters, cores removed
- 1 onion, diced
- 2 red peppers, diced
- 2 cloves of garlic, peeled and bashed
- 1 teaspoon salt
- 1 teaspoon brown sugar
- 2 teaspoons ground cumin
- 2 teaspoons paprika
- 2 tablespoons cooking oil
- salt and pepper, to taste
- 750ml hot vegetable stock (more if needed)

1. Preheat the oven to 200°C fan. Line a large baking tray with baking parchment. Put all the ingredients, apart from the stock, on the baking tray and give everything a good mix to coat the vegetables in the spices. Roast in the oven for 30 minutes, stirring halfway through. The vegetables should be slightly charred and soft.

2. Transfer the cooked vegetables into a powerful blender along with the hot stock, blend until smooth, and add salt and pepper if needed. (Be careful blending hot liquid – it's best to blend small amounts at a time.)

3. Serve with a drizzle of olive oil and slices of Granny's brown bread.

STORAGE:
Cool and store in an airtight container in the fridge for up to 3 days.

TO FREEZE:
Freeze in labelled ziplock bags for up to 3 months.

TO DEFROST:
Defrost in the fridge overnight. Reheat in a pot or in the microwave until piping hot.

TIPS:
To cook in the air fryer, put all the ingredients, apart from the stock, into the air fryer basket and air-fry at 180°C for 20–30 minutes, shaking the basket a few times. Then continue with step 2.

To make this more budget-friendly, instead of using fresh tomatoes cook everything together in a big pot, and add 2 × 400g tins of chopped tomatoes. Bring to the boil, simmer for 30–40 minutes, then blend the soup and serve.

Prep time. **15 mins**   Cook time. **40 mins**

As the September evenings start to darken and woolly jumpers come out, the craving for pots of soup begins. This sweet potato and mildly curry-spiced soup is the perfect hug-in-a-mug during the cosy season.

Curried sweet potato & coconut soup

SERVES 4

1 tablespoon cooking oil
1 onion, diced
2 cloves of garlic, chopped or grated
2–3 teaspoons mild curry powder

750g sweet potatoes, peeled and diced
800ml hot vegetable stock
1 × 400ml tin of coconut milk
salt and pepper, to taste
naan bread, to serve

1. Warm a large wide pot on a low heat, then add the oil and the diced onions and cook on a low heat until completely soft – this will take about 10 minutes. Add the garlic and curry powder, season with salt and pepper, then stir and cook for 1–2 minutes.

2. Add the sweet potatoes and stir to coat in the curried onions. Pour in the hot stock and simmer the soup on a medium heat until the sweet potatoes are soft.

3. Add the coconut milk and blend with a processor or stick blender. Taste and season to your liking. Serve with naan bread.

STORAGE:
Cool and store in an airtight container in the fridge for up to 3 days.

TO FREEZE:
Freeze in labelled ziplock bags for up to 3 months.

TO DEFROST:
Defrost in the fridge overnight. Reheat in a pot or in the microwave until piping hot.

TIP:
The smaller you dice the onion and sweet potato the more quickly the soup will cook.

Prep time. **10 mins**   Cook time. **30 mins**

This is a deliciously creamy soup. The parsnips are soft and sweet while the apples are sharp, and together they make a wonderful bowl of velvety soup. If you like a crispy crouton, this soup is the perfect partner, and if you want to make it more filling, add a cheesy toastie.

Parsnip & apple soup

SERVES 4

2 tablespoons cooking oil
2 onions, finely chopped
2 cloves of garlic, chopped
500g parsnips, peeled and diced
2 eating apples, peeled and diced
800ml hot vegetable stock, made with 1 stock pot or stock cube
salt and pepper, to taste
homemade croûtons, to serve

1. Warm a wide, deep pot on a medium heat. Drizzle in the oil, add the onions, and cook to soften for 5–10 minutes, lower the temperature if they are browning too quickly. Add the chopped garlic and cook for a further few minutes.

2. Add the diced parsnips and apples, and pour over the hot vegetable stock. Simmer for 30 minutes, until the vegetables are completely soft.

3. Blend, then check the seasoning and add salt and pepper if needed. If the soup is too thick, add some more water or some milk to loosen. Serve the soup with the crispy croûtons.

 STORAGE:
Cool and store in an airtight container in the fridge for up to 3 days.

 TO FREEZE:
Freeze in labelled ziplock bags for up to 3 months.

 TO DEFROST:
Defrost in the fridge overnight. Reheat in a pot or in the microwave until piping hot.

 TIP:
To make quick croûtons, chop 2 slices of bread into cubes. Put them into a mixing bowl and spray lightly with oil. Air-fry for 8–10 minutes at 180°C, until the croutons are golden and crispy. Serve with the soup.

Prep time. **15 mins**   Cook time. **35 mins**

Minestrone dates back to Roman times, when the word 'minestrone' meant 'to serve'. In those days it would have been made with seasonal vegetables, pulses and sometimes meat. I like to dice the vegetables the same size as the beans and add pasta of a similar size. It is so nutritious and filling.

Minestrone soup

SERVES 6

3 tablespoons cooking oil
1 onion, finely diced
salt and pepper, to taste
1 stick of celery, finely diced (100g)
1 carrot, peeled and finely diced (100g)
1 courgette, finely diced (150g)
2 cloves of garlic, chopped
1 bay leaf
2 tablespoons tomato purée
1 × 400g tin of chopped tomatoes
1.2 litres hot vegetable stock
70g dried macaroni pasta, or a similar small pasta
1 × 400g tin of cannellini beans, drained

1. Warm a wide pot on a medium heat and add the oil and onions. Cook to soften for 5 minutes, adding some salt. Add the celery, carrot and courgette and cook for a further 5 minutes, then add the garlic and the bay leaf.

2. Stir in the tomato purée and cook for a couple of minutes. Pour in the chopped tomatoes and the hot stock.

3. Bring the soup to the boil, then add the macaroni and cook for 8 minutes. Stir in the cannellini beans. Taste the soup and add more salt and pepper if needed.

STORAGE:
Cool and store in an airtight container in the fridge for up to 3 days.

TO FREEZE:
Freeze in labelled ziplock bags for up to 3 months.

TO DEFROST:
Defrost in the fridge overnight. Reheat in a pot or in the microwave until piping hot.

TIP:
If you can't find macaroni, use dried spaghetti – just break it into small pieces.

Prep time. **15 mins** Cook time. **20 mins**

I've fond memories of my mum making us chicken noodle soup after school. I can remember the smell of the soup in the kitchen, and I loved trying to fish the little bits of spaghetti out of the bowl. I'd always ask for more. Every home should have a chicken noodle soup recipe to make, share and send off to school on cold days.

Chicken noodle soup

SERVES 4

2 tablespoons cooking oil
1 onion, peeled and finely diced
salt, to taste
2 sticks of celery, finely diced (200g)
2 large carrots, peeled and finely diced (200g)
2 cloves of garlic, finely chopped
1 bay leaf
2 chicken breasts (350g), each sliced lengthways into 3 strips
1.5 litres hot chicken stock
75g dried spaghetti, broken into small pieces
Small sprig of fresh coriander to garnish, optional

1. Warm a wide pot on a medium heat, and add the oil and onions. Cook for 5 minutes to soften, then add some salt. Add the celery and carrot and cook for a further 5 minutes, then add the garlic and the bay leaf.
2. Put the raw chicken on top of the diced vegetables and pour over the hot stock. Simmer for about 10 minutes to cook the chicken fully, then take the chicken out of the pot and set aside to cool. Remove the bay leaf too.
3. Add the broken spaghetti pieces and cook for 8 minutes. When the pasta is cooked, shred the chicken into small pieces and add back to the pot.
4. Take the pot off the heat, taste and add salt if needed. Serve up in bowls with a sprig of fresh coriander.

 STORAGE:
Cool and store in an airtight container in the fridge for up to 3 days.

 TO FREEZE:
Freeze in labelled ziplock bags for up to 3 months.

TO DEFROST:
Defrost in the fridge overnight. Reheat in a pot or in the microwave until piping hot.

 Prep time. **15 mins** Cook time. **30 mins**

SMOOTHIES & SMOOTHIE POPS

ALL MAKE 2 GLASSES OR 4 ICE POPS

I wouldn't be without my smoothie-blender! Smoothies are a great way to add lots of variety and a mix of fruit to your child's diet, and I always have a stash of frozen fruit ready to grab for a quick smoothie in the morning.

Here are some optional add-ins. If you are introducing them to kids for the first time, add very small amounts to start off with: oats, chia seeds, flax seeds, nuts, seeds, nut butters and seed butters.

Mango tango

Totally tropical

Blueberry delight

Strawberry dream

Mango tango

Mango gives a delicious flavour and a great colour too. This smoothie has lots of vitamin C, making it especially good for the winter months.

150g frozen mango chunks
1 apple, peeled and sliced, or 1 banana, peeled
200ml orange juice
a dash of vanilla/honey (optional)

Blend all the ingredients together and serve.

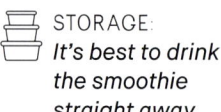 STORAGE:
It's best to drink the smoothie straight away.

 TO FREEZE:
This smoothie recipe can become a smoothie pop. Pour into silicone moulds and freeze overnight. Store in labelled ziplock bags until needed.

Totally tropical

This is my daughter's favourite smoothie – she loves pineapple! It's delicious any time, but especially good on a hot summer's day.

100g frozen pineapple chunks
1 apple, peeled and sliced, or 1 banana, peeled
1 tablespoon oats
200ml coconut milk or regular milk

Blend all the ingredients together and serve.

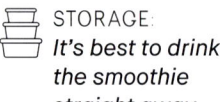 STORAGE:
It's best to drink the smoothie straight away.

 TO FREEZE:
This smoothie recipe can become a smoothie pop. Pour into silicone moulds and freeze overnight. Store in labelled ziplock bags until needed.

Prep times. **5 mins**

Strawberry dream

My son always asks for a strawberry smoothie – it's his favourite – and I can whip this up in a couple of minutes. Sometimes, instead of milk, I add some high-protein yoghurt or kefir for added gut-friendly cultures.

150g frozen strawberries
1 banana, peeled
200ml milk
1 teaspoon honey
½ teaspoon vanilla extract (optional)

Blend all the ingredients together and serve.

STORAGE:
It's best to drink the smoothie straight away.

TO FREEZE:
This smoothie recipe can become a smoothie pop. Pour into silicone moulds and freeze overnight. Store in labelled ziplock bags until needed.

Blueberry delight

Blueberries are a great source of antioxidants and help to protect the body's cells. This makes a nice thick smoothie, great for a busy school morning.

100g frozen blueberries
1 small apple, peeled and sliced, or 1 banana, peeled
100ml yoghurt
100ml milk
1 teaspoon chia seeds
1 tablespoon maple syrup
½ teaspoon vanilla extract

Blend all the ingredients together and serve.

STORAGE:
It's best to drink the smoothie straight away.

TO FREEZE:
This smoothie recipe can become a smoothie pop. Pour into silicone moulds and freeze overnight. Store in labelled ziplock bags until needed.

Image on page 96

Prep times. **5 mins**

Baby spinach is mild enough that you can add it to smoothies and get away with it! Spinach is rich in iron, and served with orange juice it's easier for the body to absorb – a great one to serve with breakfast.

Green hulk

20g baby spinach
1 banana, frozen in pieces
100ml orange juice

100ml yoghurt
100ml milk
1 teaspoon flaxseed

1. Blend all the ingredients together and serve.

STORAGE:
It's best to drink the smoothie straight away.

TO FREEZE:
This smoothie recipe can become a smoothie pop. Pour into silicone moulds and freeze overnight. Store in labelled ziplock bags until needed.

Prep time. **5 mins**

Chapter 5

Slow Cooker Dinners

This a hearty, tasty and comforting dish, ideal for the cowboys and cowgirls in your life! Beans and sausages are the perfect pair for a tasty midweek supper, and it's also a budget-friendly meal if you're trying to keep food costs low.

Imagine a cold wintry Wednesday when it's damp and dreary and everyone's coming home to a warm house with a cosy fire. The first smell they get as they open the door is this comforting slow-cooker casserole... perfect.

'Cowboy supper' sausage & bean casserole

SERVES 4

- 1–2 tablespoons cooking oil
- 6 sausages, cut into quarters (450g)
- 2 onions, finely chopped
- 4 carrots, peeled and cut into 2cm cubes
- 1 medium sweet potato, peeled and cut into 2cm cubes
- 2 teaspoons smoked paprika
- 1 bay leaf
- 1 × 400g tin of chopped tomatoes
- 1 tablespoon tomato purée
- 600ml hot beef stock
- 1 × 400g tin of cannellini beans, drained
- chopped fresh parsley, to serve

1. Heat the oil in a frying pan and brown the sausages all over, then put them into the slow cooker. This step is important because the sausages won't brown in the slow cooker. If you have time, brown the onions in the frying pan too, as this will give a better flavour to the finished dish.
2. Add all the rest of the ingredients except the cannellini beans and parsley to the slow cooker, and cook either on high for 3 hours or on low for 6 hours.
3. Add the drained beans 20 minutes before the end of the cooking time. Taste and adjust the seasoning if needed.
4. Serve with crusty bread and a sprinkling of fresh parsley.

STORAGE:
Once cooked and cooled, store in an airtight container in the fridge for up to 3 days.

TO FREEZE:
To save space in your freezer, portion the cooked and cooled bean casserole and freeze in labelled ziplock bags for up to 3 months.

TO DEFROST:
Defrost overnight in the fridge. Reheat in a pot or in the microwave until piping hot.

Prep time. **20 mins**   Cook time. **3–6 hours**

I've always loved adding Mexican-inspired flavours to the weekly meal plan. I've been making a version of this chilli for over ten years now. Chorizo is a Spanish-style sausage, not necessarily authentic to chilli but it's full of flavour and makes a delicious addition to this recipe. You can decide how much chilli powder to add, or if you have small kids you can leave it out and serve the dish with some spicy jalapenos on the side.

Beef & chorizo chilli con carne

SERVES 4

- 2 tablespoons cooking oil
- 500g beef mince (I use 10% fat)
- 1 onion, finely chopped
- 100g chorizo, diced (I use mild chorizo)
- 1 stick of celery, finely chopped
- 1 red pepper, diced
- 2 cloves of garlic, finely chopped
- 2 teaspoons ground cumin
- 2 teaspoons smoked paprika
- 1–2 teaspoons chilli powder (optional)
- 1 teaspoon salt
- 2 tablespoons tomato purée
- 1 bay leaf
- 1 × 400g tin of chopped tomatoes
- 300ml hot beef stock
- 1 × 400g tin of kidney beans, drained

1. Heat the oil in a frying pan and brown the beef mince. If you have time, fry the onions and chorizo too, as this will give a better flavour to the dish.
2. Put everything into the slow cooker, except the kidney beans, and mix well. Cook either on high for 4 hours or on low for 8 hours.
3. 30 minutes before the end of the cooking time, add the kidney beans. Taste and adjust the seasoning if needed.
4. Serve with boiled rice.

STORAGE:
Once cooked and cooled, store in an airtight container in the fridge for up to 3 days.

TO FREEZE:
To save space in your freezer, portion the cooked and cooled chilli and freeze in labelled ziplock bags for up to 3 months.

TO DEFROST:
Defrost overnight in the fridge. Reheat in a pan on the stove or in the microwave until piping hot.

Prep time. 20 mins   Cook time. 4–8 hours

I made dahl for years in my old job. We would make a large pot every few days and serve it with rice and cucumber yoghurt. Such a filling dish – it was always really popular. This is not an authentic dahl recipe but it's an easy and tasty version. It's an especially great one to make from store-cupboard ingredients.

Red lentil dahl

SERVES 4

- 1 onion, finely diced
- 1 tablespoon olive oil
- 2 cloves of garlic, finely chopped
- 2 teaspoons finely chopped fresh ginger
- 3 teaspoons curry powder
- 1 teaspoon mustard seeds
- 1 teaspoon ground turmeric
- 1 teaspoon chilli powder (optional)
- 2 carrots, peeled and finely diced
- 400g dried split red lentils, rinsed in cold water
- 1 × 400g tin of chopped tomatoes
- 500–700ml hot vegetable stock
- salt and pepper, to taste
- juice of ½ a lemon
- yoghurt and naan bread, to serve

1. If you have time, cook the diced onion in a frying pan with the oil until soft, then add the garlic, ginger, curry powder, mustard seeds, turmeric and chilli powder (if using) and cook for a further few minutes – doing this really makes for a tastier dahl. Transfer to the slow cooker. But if you are short of time, just put everything straight into the slow cooker.
2. Add the carrots, red lentils, chopped tomatoes, stock, salt and pepper. Cook either on high for 3 hours or on low for 6 hours. If the dahl appears dry, add more stock.
3. Taste the dahl, add the lemon juice and adjust the seasoning if needed.
4. Serve with yoghurt and warm naan bread.

 STORAGE:
Once cooked and cooled, store in an airtight container in the fridge for up to 3 days.

 TO FREEZE:
To save space in your freezer, portion the cooked and cooled dahl and freeze in labelled ziplock bags for up to 3 months.

 TO DEFROST:
Defrost overnight in the fridge. Reheat in a pan or in the microwave until piping hot.

 TIP:
Dahl usually has a soupy consistency, so add more stock at the end if you wish.

Prep time. **15 mins** Cook time. **3–6 hours**

I absolutely love making veggie curries in the slow cooker. The vegetables soak up the curry spices, and adding some pulses makes it super-nutritious too. This is a great one to make if you have odd bits of veggies lying around in the fridge drawer, and can reduce food waste.

If your kids like to take a flask to school you could add some hot veggie curry with a little pot of yoghurt and homemade naan on the side … perfect for a warm, tasty lunch!

Chickpea & butternut squash curry

SERVES 4-6

- 2 tablespoons olive oil
- 1 onion, chopped
- 3 cloves of garlic, chopped
- 2 teaspoons grated fresh ginger
- 1 teaspoon salt
- ½ teaspoon ground turmeric
- 2 tablespoons curry powder
- ½ teaspoon ground cumin
- ½ a butternut squash (250g), peeled and cut into 2cm cubes
- 1 medium sweet potato (250g), peeled and cut into 2cm cubes
- 1 × 400ml tin of good quality full-fat coconut milk
- 1 × 400g tin of chickpeas, drained and rinsed
- 125ml water
- 1 large handful of baby spinach
- juice of ½ a lemon
- salt and pepper, to taste

TO SERVE
boiled rice and fresh coriander

1. If you have time, heat the oil in a frying pan and cook the onion until soft, then add the garlic, ginger, salt, turmeric, curry powder and cumin and cook for a further few minutes. Then transfer everything into the slow cooker. If you are short of time, just put all the above straight into the slow cooker.

2. Add the butternut squash, sweet potato, coconut milk and water. Cook on high for 2–3 hours or on low for 4–5 hours. The time may vary, just check that the veg are cooked through.

3. Stir in the chickpeas 30 minutes from the end of the cooking time, and add the spinach and lemon juice for the last 2 minutes. Taste and adjust the seasoning if needed.

4. Serve up the curry with boiled rice and garnish with fresh coriander.

STORAGE:
Once cooked and cooled, store in an airtight container in the fridge for up to 3 days.

TO FREEZE:
To save space in your freezer, portion the cooked and cooled curry and freeze in labelled ziplock bags for up to 3 months.

TO DEFROST:
Defrost overnight in the fridge. Reheat in a pan or in the microwave until piping hot.

Prep time. **20 mins**   Cook time. **2–5 hours**

Sometimes you just need to load up on the veggies and lentils, and for those times this is the perfect dish. It works great with pasta, but also in a lasagne if you fancy giving that a go too. I'll be honest, getting my kids to accept pulses in their meals has been slow, but with time they are learning to like them. If you're not there yet, keep trying.

Veggie bolognaise

SERVES 4–6

- 2 tablespoons cooking oil
- 1 onion, finely chopped
- 2 cloves of garlic, finely chopped
- 2 carrots, peeled and diced
- 200g button mushrooms, diced
- 1 × 400g tin of chopped tomatoes
- 150ml hot vegetable stock
- 2 tablespoons tomato purée
- 2 teaspoons honey
- 1 bay leaf
- salt and pepper, to taste
- 2 × 400g tins of green lentils, drained and rinsed
- juice of ½ a lemon

TO SERVE
cooked pasta
grated cheese
garlic bread

1. Heat a frying pan, and add the oil and onions. Cook on a low heat until soft, 5–10 minutes, then add the garlic and cook for a further few minutes. Transfer to the slow cooker.
2. Add the rest of the ingredients to the slow cooker except the lentils and lemon juice. Cook on high for 3 hours or on low for 6 hours.
3. 30 minutes from the end of the cooking time, stir in the cooked lentils. Finish with the lemon juice, tasting and adjusting the seasoning if needed.
4. Serve with cooked pasta, cheese and garlic bread.

STORAGE:
Once cooked and cooled, store in an airtight container in the fridge for up to 3 days.

TO FREEZE:
To save space in your freezer, portion the cooked and cooled bolognaise and freeze in labelled ziplock bags for up to 3 months.

TO DEFROST:
Defrost overnight in the fridge. Reheat in a pan or in the microwave until piping hot.

TIP:
The lemon juice helps to lift the flavours at the end of the cooking time – try adding it to soups and stews as well.

Pulled pork works so well in the slow cooker, and drenched in BBQ sauce it makes the best sandwich. We used to cook pork shoulder slowly overnight in the restaurant I worked in, and it would taste incredible the next day. The meat is so tender and pulls apart perfectly. The BBQ sauce is necessary, but you can decide whether you want to make it or buy it.

BBQ pulled pork on soft bread rolls

MAKES 8

2 tablespoons smoked paprika
1 tablespoon ground cumin
1 teaspoon ground black pepper
1kg pork loin or pork shoulder
1½ teaspoons salt
100ml apple juice

FOR THE BBQ SAUCE
500g tomato ketchup
100ml apple cider vinegar
100ml water, or the pork juices
40g honey
50g brown sugar
1 teaspoon Dijon mustard
2 teaspoons paprika
1 teaspoon Worcestershire sauce
salt and pepper, to taste

TO SERVE
8 x soft bread rolls
sliced cucumber
gem lettuce

1. Marinate the pork first. Mix the smoked paprika, cumin and black pepper in a small bowl. Put the pork on a plate and pierce the meat deeply all over with a sharp knife – this will help to get the seasoning into the meat. Coat the pork all over with the spice mix, then cover and leave in the fridge to marinate for at least 30 minutes, or overnight if possible.

2. Preheat the slow cooker and add in the pork. Sprinkle it with salt and pour in the apple juice. Cook on high for 4 hours or on low for 8 hours. The meat should be tender and should pull apart when it's cooked.

3. To make the BBQ sauce, put all the ingredients into a pot and simmer on a low heat for 40 minutes, until the sauce is smooth and shiny.

4. When the pork is ready, shred the meat using two forks. Mix through the hot sauce and serve on soft white bread buns with the sliced cucumber and gem lettuce.

STORAGE:
Once cooked and cooled, store the pulled pork in the sauce in an airtight container in the fridge for up to 3 days.

TO FREEZE:
Freeze the cooked and cooled pulled pork and sauce together in a labelled ziplock bag for up to 3 months.

TO DEFROST:
Defrost overnight in the fridge. Reheat in a pan or in the microwave until piping hot.

 Prep time. **20 mins plus time to marinate**   Cook time. **4-8 hours**

Slow-cooked meatballs are the absolute best – they are soft and take on the flavours of the sauce. I've been making spaghetti and meatballs for my kids since they were babies.

When my daughter was small she used to play 'Find the meatball'. I'd hide the meatballs under the spaghetti and sauce and she would hunt for them and cry out when she found one. Such a fond food memory.

Saucy meatballs with pasta

SERVES 4–6

FOR THE MEATBALLS (MAKES 16)
500g beef mince (10% fat)
50g breadcrumbs
1 teaspoon paprika
1 teaspoon ground cumin
½ teaspoon oregano
½ teaspoon salt

FOR THE SAUCE
1 onion, finely diced
2 cloves of garlic, grated
1 tablespoon tomato purée
2 × 400g tins of chopped tomatoes
1 beef stockpot or cube, crumbled
salt and pepper, to taste

TO SERVE:
cooked spaghetti
grated Parmesan

1. Preheat the oven to 180°C. To make the meatballs, put all the ingredients into a bowl and mix really well. Divide into 16 balls and roll them in the palms of your hands, then place them on a greased baking tray. Cook in the oven for 15 minutes to brown all over, or brown them in a frying pan.

2. To make the sauce, heat a frying pan and add some oil, then add the onions and cook until soft, adding the garlic for the last minute. Put the onions, garlic, tomato purée, tinned tomatoes, beef stockpot and salt and pepper into the slow cooker.

3. When the meatballs are browned, add them to the slow cooker. Cook for 4 hours on low or 2½ hours on high. When the time is up, check the seasoning and adjust if needed.

4. Serve with spaghetti and grated Parmesan.

STORAGE:
Once cooked and cooled, store in an airtight container in the fridge for up to 3 days.

TO FREEZE:
To save space in your freezer, portion the cooked and cooled meatballs and sauce and freeze in labelled ziplock bags for up to 3 months.

TO DEFROST:
Defrost overnight in the fridge. Reheat in a pan or in the microwave until piping hot.

TIP:
The meatballs need to be browned first, as they won't brown in the slow cooker.

Prep time. **20 mins**   Cook time. **2½–3 hours**

Does your family love a takeaway? We do, but it can be expensive, which is why I love to make our favourite butter chicken curry for a Saturday night. I pop it on to cook early and it's ready by teatime. Then it's dinner, followed by a movie and popcorn, and everyone's happy! If I'm organized I will make it during the week and freeze it to enjoy at the weekend too! That's a real treat, because all I need to make on the day is the rice.

Butter chicken curry

SERVES 4

FOR THE CHICKEN MARINADE:
- 120ml plain yoghurt
- 1 tablespoon lemon juice
- 2 tablespoons garam masala
- 3 tablespoons curry powder
- 1 teaspoon cumin
- salt and pepper, to taste
- 4 chicken breasts (800g), diced

FOR THE SAUCE:
- 100g butter, cut into small pieces
- 1 large onion, finely chopped
- 4 cloves of garlic, grated
- 2 teaspoons grated fresh ginger
- 1 × 400g tin of chopped tomatoes
- 2 tablespoons tomato purée
- 1 tablespoon honey (optional, to balance acidity)
- ½ × 400g tin of coconut milk, just the thick cream from the top
- salt and pepper, to taste

TO SERVE:
- cooked rice
- chopped coriander
- naan (optional)

1. For the marinade, combine the yoghurt, lemon juice, garam masala, curry powder, cumin, salt, and pepper in a large mixing bowl. Add the chicken pieces, making sure they are well coated. Cover and refrigerate for 30 minutes.

2. Melt half the butter over a medium heat in a large frying pan. Add the chopped onions and cook until golden brown, about 5–7 minutes. Add the garlic and ginger, and cook for another 1–2 minutes until fragrant. Transfer the mixture to the slow cooker along with the chicken.

3. Pour in the tinned tomatoes, and add the tomato purée and honey (if using). Scatter the remaining butter evenly over the top. Cook on low for 4 hours or on high for 2 hours.

4. About 30 minutes before serving, stir in the coconut cream. Taste and adjust the seasoning as needed. Continue cooking on a low heat until the sauce is thickened and the chicken is tender.

5. Serve with cooked rice and garnish with chopped coriander. Add a naan if you fancy!

STORAGE:
Once cooked and cooled, store in an airtight container in the fridge for up to 3 days.

FREEZE:
To save space in your freezer, portion the cooked and cooled butter chicken curry and freeze in labelled ziplock bags for up to 3 months.

TO DEFROST:
Defrost overnight in the fridge. Reheat in a pan or in the microwave until piping hot.

TIP:
if you like a spicy curry, use a medium or hot curry powder, if it's for small kids use a mild curry powder.

Prep time. **20 mins**   Cook time. **2–4 hours**

To me this is pure comfort food, and it makes a great Sunday family dinner without any of the fuss.

Lemon chicken reminds me of a weekend we once had in Paris, before we had kids. I ordered it in a little restaurant in St Michel and it was served with boiled potatoes and green beans, cooked with few ingredients but full of flavour. I love to cook dishes for my family that I've had on my travels. It always evokes lovely memories and interesting conversations with the kids.

Creamy garlic & lemon chicken with buttery mash and veg

SERVES 4

4 chicken breasts
½ teaspoon salt
¼ teaspoon ground black pepper
1 teaspoon oregano
oil, for cooking
zest and juice of 1 lemon
3 cloves of garlic, chopped
100ml hot chicken stock (use ½ a stock cube)

2 tablespoons cornflour
½ teaspoon Dijon mustard
250ml double cream

TO SERVE
mashed potato (see page 146)
green beans
carrots
lemon wedges
chopped fresh parsley

1. Warm a large frying pan on a medium heat. Season the chicken breasts with salt, pepper and oregano, add some oil to the pan, and sear for about 5 minutes, until brown all over. Put the chicken breasts into the slow cooker, add the lemon juice, lemon zest and garlic, and pour in the chicken stock. Cook on low for 4 hours, or on high for 2 hours.

2. After the cooking time, remove the chicken breasts to a plate and cover to keep warm.

3. Make a paste by mixing the cornflour, mustard and a tablespoon of water in a small bowl, and pour this into a small pot. Put 2 ladles of the juices from the slow cooker into the pot of paste and whisk on a medium heat for a few minutes to cook out the cornflour, then add the cream and the rest of the juices and let it bubble and cook for a few minutes. Taste and adjust the seasoning if needed, then pour back into the slow cooker and put the chicken back too for a final 10 mins.

4. Serve with creamy mashed potato, green beans and carrots. Garnish with a lemon wedge and a sprinkle of chopped parsley.

STORAGE:
Once cooked and cooled, store in an airtight container in the fridge for up to 3 days.

TO FREEZE:
To save space in your freezer, portion the cooked and cooled chicken and sauce and freeze in labelled ziplock bags for up to 3 months.

TO DEFROST:
Defrost overnight in the fridge. Reheat in a pan or in the microwave until piping hot.

I have a soft spot for Morocco – I love its culture, colours and spices, and it's where Mike and I got engaged. A tagine is like a casserole and traditionally is slow-cooked over coals in a special pot with a tepee-like lid. This is my slow cooker version and it's very tasty indeed, with added sweetness from the dried dates.

Moroccan lamb tagine with couscous

SERVES 4

- 1½ tablespoons cooking oil
- 400g diced lamb
- 1 onion, finely diced
- 2 carrots, finely diced
- 2 sticks of celery, finely diced
- 2 cloves of garlic, chopped
- 1½ tablespoons tomato purée
- 1½ tablespoons ras el hanout
- 1½ tablespoons paprika
- salt and pepper, to taste
- 500ml beef stock
- 10 dried dates or apricots, pitted and chopped
- 1 × 400g tin of chickpeas, drained
- juice of ½ a lemon

TO SERVE:
- couscous
- Greek yoghurt
- toasted flaked almonds
- a handful of chopped parsley or coriander

1. Heat the oil in a frying pan – when it's pretty hot, add the lamb in small batches to sear and brown on all sides. Remove to a plate until needed.
2. Add the diced onion and cook for 5 minutes to soften. Add the carrots, celery and garlic and cook for a further few minutes. Stir through the tomato purée, ras el hanout, paprika, and salt and pepper to taste. Cook for a few minutes to toast the spices, being careful not to let them burn.
3. Put all this into the slow cooker along with the lamb, the beef stock and dates. Cook on high for 4–5 hours or on low for 8 hours, or until the lamb is soft and tender. When you are 30 minutes from the end of the cooking time, add the chickpeas and lemon juice.
4. Cook the couscous according to the packet instructions. Taste the tagine and adjust the seasoning if needed.
5. Serve the tagine with the couscous, yoghurt, toasted flaked almonds and some chopped parsley or coriander.

STORAGE:
Once cooked and cooled, store in an airtight container in the fridge for 3 days.

TO FREEZE:
To save space in your freezer, portion the cooked and cooled tagine and freeze in labelled ziplock bags for up to 3 months.

TO DEFROST:
Defrost overnight in the fridge. Reheat in a pan or in the microwave until piping hot.

TIP:
If you can't find ras el hanout, make your own version with: 2 teaspoons ground cumin, 2 teaspoons ground coriander, 1 teaspoon ground turmeric, ½ teaspoon ground cinnamon, ½ teaspoon chilli flakes, 1 teaspoon ground black pepper and ½ teaspoon crushed cardamom. Store any left over in an airtight jar for up to 3 months.

Prep time: **20 mins**   Cook time: **4–8 hours**

Chapter 6

Air Fryer

Chicken goujons are a family favourite! My kids nearly always order them when we're out for a meal, and I don't mind as long as they're made with real breast meat. If you make them at home you can be sure they are a good source of protein even for the pickiest eaters.

Chicken goujons with mushy peas & mashed potato

SERVES 4

4 chicken breasts

FOR THE FLOUR MIX
100g plain flour
2 teaspoons paprika,
1 teaspoon ground cumin
1 teaspoon salt
½ teaspoon ground black pepper

FOR THE EGG DIP
2 eggs, beaten
2 tablespoons milk

FOR THE CRUMB
100g panko breadcrumbs, or homemade breadcrumbs or crushed cornflakes
1 teaspoon paprika
oil, for cooking

FOR THE MUSHY PEAS
1 tablespoon butter
2 cloves of garlic, finely grated or chopped
300g frozen peas
salt and pepper
2 tablespoons cream (optional)
juice of ½ a lemon

TO SERVE
mashed potato (see page 146)

1. Slice each chicken breast into 4 long strips, to give 16 pieces in total.
2. Get yourself three separate bowls. In the first, mix all the ingredients for the flour mix, in the second, whisk the eggs and milk to make the egg dip, and in the third, stir the breadcrumbs and paprika for the crumb.
3. Coat the chicken pieces thoroughly in the flour mix, then cover with the egg dip and finally coat fully with the crumb. Put them on a large tray. Repeat with the rest of the goujons.
4. Preheat the air fryer to 180°C for 5 minutes. Spray the bottom of the basket with oil and add the chicken pieces – don't overlap them. Spray the top of the chicken with oil. Cook for 12–15 minutes, turning the pieces halfway through. Check the meat is cooked through and no pink remains.
5. Serve the chicken with the mashed potato and mushy peas.

FOR THE MUSHY PEAS
Heat the butter in a saucepan over a medium heat, then add the garlic and cook gently for a minute. Add the frozen peas and

TO FREEZE:
The raw breaded chicken goujons can be frozen on the tray, then put into labelled ziplock bags for 3 months.

The mushy peas can be fully made, cooled and frozen in suitable containers or bags for up to 3 months.

TO DEFROST:
Cook the goujons from frozen, step 4, but add 5 extra minutes to the cooking time.

Defrost the mushy peas overnight in the fridge, then heat through until piping hot and serve.

TIPS:
If your air fryer is small you may have to cook the chicken in batches.

 Prep time. **25 mins**   Cook time. **30 mins**

cook until completely soft. Lightly season everything with salt and pepper and pour in the cream (if using).

Blend the cooked pea mixture in a food processor, keeping it chunky if you wish or blending until it's a smooth purée. The mixture will still be quite thick. Add the juice of the lemon and blend again. Taste and add more salt and pepper as needed.

Breading chicken takes a bit of effort, so it's a good idea to double up this recipe and make an extra batch for the freezer.

Air Fryer

These are inspired by my son's love of burgers, cheese and apples! Pork and apple is a great combination, and the cheese gives some nice richness and flavour. Sweet potato fries are a good option for adding some fibre into the meal, and my kids like to dip them in sauce.

Pork & apple burgers with sweet potato chips

MAKES 6 SMALL BURGERS

500g pork mince
2 eating apples, peeled and grated
70g Cheddar cheese, grated
50g panko breadcrumbs
2 tablespoons milk
salt and pepper

FOT THE SWEET POTATO CHIPS
2 medium sweet potatoes, peeled and sliced
½ teaspoon salt
½ teaspoon cornflour
½ teaspoon smoked paprika
1 tablespoon cooking oil

TO SERVE
super-soft bread rolls (page 203)
lettuce
tomato slices

1. Put the pork mince, grated apples, Cheddar cheese, panko breadcrumbs, milk and a pinch of salt and pepper into a bowl and mix together.
2. Shape into 6 burger patties with your hands. Use a burger press if you have one, or a large cookie cutter to make them nice and round.
3. Preheat the air fryer to 180°C. Place the burgers in the basket, using a liner if you wish. Cook for 12 minutes, turning them halfway through.

FOR THE SWEET POTATO CHIPS

Preheat the air fryer to 180°C. Cut the sweet potatoes into chips 1cm thick. Place them in a mixing bowl.

Sprinkle over the salt, cornflour and paprika, toss and drizzle with oil, then toss again.

Cook in the air fryer for 12 minutes, shaking halfway through.

TO FREEZE:
After shaping the pork burgers, put them on a tray, cover and put the tray into the freezer. Once frozen, transfer them to a labelled ziplock bag and put them back into the freezer straight away. Freeze for up to 3 months.

To freeze the chips, put the seasoned and oiled raw sweet potatoes flat on a tray and put the tray into the freezer. Once frozen, transfer them to a labelled ziplock bag and freeze for up to 3 months. To cook from frozen, add a few extra minutes if needed.

TO DEFROST:
Defrost overnight and cook in the air fryer the next day. To cook from frozen, add 5 more minutes to the cooking time.

Prep time. 20 mins   Cook time. 25 mins

Growing up in the 80s in rural Ireland was really different to the Ireland of today. Chips were a real novelty for us. We'd get them at the chipper a couple of times a year if we were lucky. And if we had them at home, they were always homemade and cooked in the deep-fat fryer! These chips taste great, and you can prep them and have them in the freezer ready to go!

Homemade chips, eggs & beans

SERVES 4

700g potatoes (I like to use Roosters, 4 big ones)
1½ tablespoons cornflour
2 tablespoons frying oil (use your favourite neutral-tasting oil – such as rapeseed, sunflower or vegetable)
1 teaspoon salt
1 teaspoon paprika

TO SERVE
4 eggs
oil, for cooking
baked beans

1. Peel the potatoes and slice into chips (about 1cm thick). Rinse in a bowl of cold water, then drain and pat dry.
2. Put the chips into a bowl and toss with the cornflour until coated.
3. Next add the oil, salt and paprika and toss again so they're evenly coated.
4. Place in the air fryer and cook at 180°C for 20–25 minutes, shaking every 5 minutes. For a crispier chip, increase the temperature to 200°C for the last 5 minutes.
5. Serve with fried eggs and baked beans.

TO FREEZE:
After step 3 the chips can be frozen raw. Place them flat and separated on a tray, then put the tray into the freezer. Once frozen, put the chips into a labelled ziplock bag and freeze for up to 3 months. Cook from frozen as per step 4 – the cooking time will be similar, but add a couple of minutes if needed.

Prep time. **20 mins**   Cook time. **25 mins**

Fajitas are so quick and easy to make, and they're full of flavour. They make a great family-style meal, where everything can be put on the table and everyone can help themselves.

It can be hard to get the kids to the dinner table at times. One thing I found that works in the winter months is lighting a few candles and turning off the lights.

Each of the kids has their own candle that we light together, and after dinner they get to blow them out. It creates a lovely intimate atmosphere and they stay at the table a little bit longer.

Mexican beef fajitas

MAKES 8

2 sirloin steaks (400g), cut into strips
2 teaspoons oil
1–2 tablespoons fajita seasoning
½ a yellow pepper, sliced into strips
½ a red pepper, sliced into strips
1 small red onion, sliced
salt and pepper

TO SERVE
8 small soft tortilla wraps
sour cream
lime wedges
fresh coriander

1. Preheat the air fryer to 190°C. Put the steak strips into a bowl, add 1 teaspoon of oil and the fajita seasoning, mix well, then set aside.
2. Put the pepper strips and onion slices into a separate bowl and add 1 teaspoon of oil and a pinch of salt and pepper. Put them into the air fryer basket and cook for 4 minutes.
3. Add the steak strips to the vegetables in the air fryer and cook for 5 minutes, then shake the basket and cook for 4 minutes more.
4. Toast the tortillas in a dry frying pan, or wrap them in tin foil and warm them through in the air fryer for a couple of minutes.
5. Divide the beef and peppers between the warm tortilla wraps, and dollop on some sour cream, a squeeze of lime and a scattering of fresh coriander leaves.

STORAGE:
If there is any beef left over, let it cool and store it in the fridge for up to 3 days. Reheat until piping hot before serving.

TO FREEZE:
Slice and marinate the steak strips, place them in a labelled ziplock bag. Chop the peppers and onion and place in a second labelled ziplock bag. To keep them together, put an elastic band around them and freeze for up to 3 months.

TO DEFROST:
Defrost in the fridge overnight. To cook, follow the cooking instructions from step 2.

TIP:
You can change up the meat and swap out the beef for chicken breast, pork loin or lamb.

To make your own fajita seasoning, mix 2 teaspoons of sweet paprika with 1 teaspoon each of ground cumin, ground coriander, cayenne, garlic powder and oregano.

Prep time. **15 mins**   Cook time. **20 mins**

If you're looking to add more meat-free meals to the weekly menu, try these. Beanie patties are a family favourite here. They are crispy on the outside, and soft and full of flavour on the inside. This is also a great store-cupboard recipe.

Easy beanie patties

MAKES 6 SMALL PATTIES

oil, for cooking
1 onion, finely diced
2 cloves of garlic, grated or finely chopped
1 teaspoon ground cumin
1 tablespoon chopped herbs (thyme and rosemary, fresh or dried)
1 tablespoon tomato purée
1 × 400g tin of black beans, rinsed and drained
1 egg, beaten
a squeeze of lemon juice
salt and pepper
a splash of Worcestershire sauce (optional)
100g panko breadcrumbs (or homemade breadcrumbs)
a little flour (optional)

TO SERVE
lettuce
tomato slices
red onion slices

1. Heat a tablespoon of oil in a frying pan, add the diced onion and cook gently for about 5 minutes until softened. Add the garlic and cook for a further 2 minutes. Add the cumin, herbs and tomato purée and cook for 3 minutes. Transfer to a plate and set aside to cool.

2. Once cooled, put the onion mix into a processor with the black beans, egg, lemon juice, salt, pepper and the Worcestershire sauce (if using). Blend, then add the breadcrumbs and blend again – the mix should be coarse.

3. Scoop out the mix, and use your hands to shape it into 6 patties. If they are sticky, use a small amount of flour to coat and shape them.

4. Preheat the air fryer to 180°C. Spray the air fryer basket or use a liner, then add the patties, lightly spray with oil and cook for 10 minutes, turning halfway through the cooking time. Serve with a simple salad.

TO FREEZE:
Freeze the prepared, uncooked patties on a tray, then transfer them to a labelled ziplock bag and freeze for up to 3 months. Cook in the air fryer from frozen, following step 4, adding 3–5 extra minutes of cooking time.

TIPS:
To make your own breadcrumbs, whizz 2 slices of old bread in a food processor.

If your air fryer basket is small, cook the patties in batches.

Prep time. **15 mins**   Cook time. **15 mins**

I like to buy turkey mince to mix things up now and again. It's a nice change from red meat and a leaner, healthier option, too. Because these meatballs are low in fat and less juicy, it's good to serve them in a sauce. My kids love a meatball sub roll for dinner, and I love making this because it is so quick and easy!

Quick turkey meatballs on a sub roll with tomato sauce

SERVES 4

400g turkey mince
25g panko breadcrumbs
1 clove of garlic, grated or finely chopped
1 teaspoon salt
1 teaspoon paprika
1 egg
2 tablespoons milk
spray oil

TO SERVE

sub rolls or bread rolls
tomato sauce (homemade or shop-bought – for quick tomato sauce, see page 158)
grated cheese

1. To make the meatballs, put all the ingredients, except the oil, into a mixing bowl, mix well, then divide and roll into 12 even balls.
2. Preheat the air fryer to 170°C. Lightly spray the basket with oil and add the balls, working in batches if the basket is small. Air-fry for 10–12 minutes, shaking the basket halfway through.
3. Heat the tomato sauce and add the cooked turkey meatballs. Put 3 meatballs and some sauce on each roll, coat in sauce, and top with grated cheese.

 TO FREEZE:
Freeze the raw turkey balls on a tray, then transfer into labelled ziplock bags and freeze for 3 months.

 TO DEFROST:
Defrost in the fridge overnight or cook from frozen, according to step 2, but add 3–5 extra minutes to the cooking time.

Prep time. **10 mins**   Cook time. **15 mins**

Crispy chicken in a sweet sticky sauce is the kind of recipe you'll come back to again and again, and it can be served with rice, noodles or even chips. It makes a really tasty fakeaway, perfect for the weekend.

Crispy sweet chilli chicken with soy noodles

SERVES 4

- 60g cornflour or plain flour
- 1 teaspoon paprika
- 1 teaspoon ground cumin
- ½ teaspoon salt
- ½ teaspoon pepper
- 3 chicken breasts, cut into bite-size cubes (500g)
- 1 egg, beaten
- 100g panko breadcrumbs
- a good amount of oil, for frying

FOR THE CHILLI SAUCE
- 100ml sweet chilli sauce
- 50ml light soy sauce
- 30ml rice wine vinegar, plain white vinegar or apple cider vinegar
- 1 clove of garlic, freshly grated
- 1 teaspoon freshly grated ginger

TO SERVE:
- Chinese noodles, 1 nest per person
- light soy sauce
- raw carrot and spring onion strips

1. Put the cornflour, paprika, cumin, salt and pepper into a bowl and stir to combine. Add the chicken strips and coat in the flour mix. Dip the floured chicken into the egg, then coat in the panko breadcrumbs. Place on a baking tray and repeat with the rest of the chicken.

2. Spray or drizzle the breadcrumbed chicken pieces with oil – this is to make sure they go golden brown and crispy.

3. Preheat the air fryer to 180°C. Add the chicken pieces and cook for 12–15 minutes, shaking the basket halfway through. If the basket is small, cook in batches. Check that the chicken is cooked completely all the way through. Put all the cooked chicken on a plate.

4. To make the sauce, combine all the ingredients in a bowl. Warm a large frying pan on a medium heat and pour in the sauce mix. Simmer and bubble for a few minutes to thicken. Add the cooked chicken pieces, coat in the sauce and heat through.

5. Cook the noodles as per the packet instructions, then toss through some light soy sauce and the carrot and spring onion strips. Serve with the crispy sweet chilli chicken.

 TO FREEZE:
Place the raw breaded chicken pieces flat on a tray without overlapping. Cover the tray with foil or cling film and freeze. Once frozen, transfer the chicken to a labelled ziplock bag and freeze for up to 3 months.

 TO DEFROST:
Defrost in the fridge overnight or cook from frozen, adding a few more minutes to the cooking time.

Prep time. **15 mins**   Cook time. **25 mins**

I will always order falafel if we are eating out and it's on the menu! I think it's such a great veggie option and it's full of flavour. Purists make it with soaked raw chickpeas, not tinned, but this way is quicker and I love a shortcut. You can serve the falafels, pitas and salad separately and let everyone build their own.

Falafel, herb yoghurt & pita breads

SERVES 4

- 1 × 400g tin of chickpeas, drained and dried
- 1 tablespoon chopped fresh coriander
- zest of ½ a lemon
- ½ a small red onion, chopped
- 2 cloves of garlic, roughly chopped
- ½ teaspoon ground coriander
- ½ teaspoon paprika
- ½ teaspoon ground cumin
- ½ teaspoon salt
- 1½ tablespoons plain flour or chickpea flour
- oil spray

TO SERVE
- pita bread
- herb yoghurt (see tip)

1. Put all the ingredients, except the oil, into a food processor and pulse to combine. Divide into 12 portions and roll each one into a ball, gently pushing down to flatten them.
2. Preheat the air fryer to 200°C for 5 minutes. Spray the basket with oil or use a liner, then add the falafel balls and give them a spray too. Air-fry for 8–10 minutes. If your air fryer basket is small, work in batches.
3. Serve warm, with pita bread and herb yoghurt.

TO FREEZE:
Freeze the cooked falafel balls, once cooled, in labelled ziplock bags for up to 3 months.

TO DEFROST:
Defrost overnight or reheat from frozen. To reheat defrosted falafel, air-fry at 180°C for 6–8 minutes. If cooking from frozen, air-fry at 180°C for 10–12 minutes.

TIP:
To make herb yoghurt, mix together 200ml of plain yoghurt, the zest and juice of ½ a lemon, 2 tablespoons of finely chopped fresh dill or parsley, 1 small clove of garlic, finely grated, salt and pepper.

Prep time. **15 mins**   Cook time. **15 mins**

Salmon is a great source of omega 3 and great for the whole family. We call fish 'brain food' in our house, so whoever eats the most fish has the most brains. It doesn't always convince my picky eater, but we laugh about it and hope one day he'll enjoy it too!

Cooking salmon in the air fryer is so quick and easy, especially after a busy day. This dinner is ideal if you are pushed for time, as you can have it on the table in just 30 minutes.

Soy & honey salmon with rice & greens

SERVES 4

4 fillets of salmon (500g)
4 tablespoons soy sauce
2 tablespoons honey or maple syrup

TO SERVE
boiled rice
steamed broccoli
toasted sesame seeds

1. Put the salmon fillets into a wide bowl or tray. Pour over the soy sauce and honey.
2. Cover the bowl and put into the fridge to marinate for 15–30 minutes (leave for up to 1 hour if you have the time).
3. Preheat the air fryer to 200°C. Line with baking parchment, then pop the 4 fillets in, skin side down.
4. Cook for 8–10 minutes, depending on the thickness of the fillets.
5. Serve with boiled rice, steamed broccoli and toasted sesame seeds.

To oven cook: Preheat the oven to 180°C fan and cook for about 12–16 minutes.

TO FREEZE:
It's a good idea to keep raw unmarinated salmon fillets in the freezer for this recipe. Store the fillets in labelled ziplock bags.

TO DEFROST:
Defrost the salmon in the fridge overnight or on the worktop for an hour or two. Once defrosted, go to step 1.

TIP:
I usually peel off the salmon skin and discard it. If you want crispy skin, don't use the baking parchment and cook the fillets skin side up, making sure to preheat the air fryer for about 5 minutes so the fish doesn't stick to the basket.

Prep time. 10 mins   Cook time. 20 mins plus time to marinate

Meatloaf is a really popular American family dish. I remember it was mentioned in the American TV comedy show *Rosanne* back in the 80s! If you haven't tried it before, you really should. Meatloaf is such an easy recipe to put together and cook. We love beef burgers, and meatloaf is like a giant burger cut into slices. It makes a great family meal.

Meatloaf with tomato sauce & baby potatoes

SERVES 6

FOR THE MEATLOAF
600g beef mince (10% fat)
1 small onion, finely chopped
1 large egg
30ml milk
100g panko breadcrumbs
3 tablespoons Parmesan cheese
1 fat clove of garlic, grated
1 tablespoon ketchup
1 tablespoon Worcestershire sauce
1 teaspoon dried oregano
1 teaspoon salt

FOR THE GLAZE
120g tomato ketchup

TO SERVE
baby potatoes
green beans

1. Measure the air fryer basket to make sure the meatloaf will fit. Preheat the air fryer to 170°C.
2. Mix all the ingredients for the meatloaf together in a big mixing bowl, using your hands if you need to. Make it into a big smooth oval shape that will fit the basket.
3. Add a liner to the air fryer if you're worried the meatloaf might stick. Carefully place the meatloaf in the air fryer. Air-fry at 170°C for 50 minutes, turning halfway through.
4. While the meatloaf cooks, boil the baby potatoes until soft in a pan of salted water. And a few minutes from the end, boil the green beans in a small pan of salted boiling water.
5. To glaze, pour 120g of your favourite ketchup over the top. Leave to rest for 15 minutes, then slice and serve with the baby potatoes and green beans.

TO FREEZE UNCOOKED:
Wrap the prepared meatloaf in foil and freeze in in a large labelled ziplock bag for up to 3 months.

TO DEFROST UNCOOKED:
Defrost in the fridge overnight and continue from step 3.

TO FREEZE COOKED:
You can also freeze the cooked meatloaf. I find it best to slice it and freeze the slices flat in labelled ziplock bags.

TO DEFROST COOKED:
Defrost overnight in the fridge and reheat in the air fryer for 10 minutes.

Prep time. **20 mins**   Cook time. **50 mins**

Chapter 7

Family Pies & Delicious Dishes

I spent a couple of years backpacking in Australia in my twenties. We ate on a budget but I remember the food being a real fusion of familiar dishes. This pie is a great example. My Aussie friend sent me her recipe last year and we've been loving it ever since.

Beef stroganoff cottage pie

SERVES 6

- 2 tablespoons olive oil, for cooking
- 800g stewing beef, diced
- salt and pepper, to taste
- 1 large onion, diced
- 2 cloves of garlic, chopped
- 2 tablespoons plain flour
- 2 tablespoons tomato purée
- 2 teaspoons paprika
- 1 teaspoon brown sugar
- 1 teaspoon Dijon mustard
- 600ml hot beef stock
- 300g mushrooms, sliced
- 2 tablespoons sour cream
- 2 teaspoons Worcestershire sauce

FOR THE MASH
- 1 kg potatoes, peeled and diced
- 2 tablespoons butter
- 2 tablespoons milk
- 1 teaspoon salt

1. Begin by browning the beef in batches. Heat a large cast-iron casserole pot or similar and add a tablespoon of oil. When it's nice and hot, add the diced beef and a little bit of salt and pepper, brown all over, then place the beef in a heatproof bowl and repeat with the next batch.

2. Add more oil to the pan if needed, then add the onion, cooking until soft, followed by the garlic. Put the beef back into the pot, sprinkle in the flour, and stir to coat the beef. Add the tomato purée, paprika, brown sugar, Dijon mustard and another pinch of salt and pepper.

3. Pour in the stock and bring to the boil, then reduce the heat to low and put the lid on. Cook, stirring occasionally, for 1½ hours – if the beef is sticking to the pot, turn down the heat even more, but make sure it's still cooking away.

4. Add the sliced mushrooms and cook for another hour with the lid off. If the sauce is very thick, add a dash of boiling water and give it a stir. Cook until the beef is very tender, then stir in the sour cream and the Worcestershire sauce.

5. While the beef cooks, put the diced potatoes into a large pot, cover with boiling water and add a pinch of salt, then cook on a medium heat for 12–15 minutes, until cooked. Strain, return them to the pan, then add the butter, milk and salt, and mash really well.

STORAGE:
Once cooked and cooled, store in an airtight container in the fridge for up to 3 days.

TO FREEZE:
It's best to freeze the whole dish or divide it into portions and put it into labelled containers. Freeze for up to 3 months.

TO DEFROST:
Defrost overnight in the fridge. Reheat in the oven at 180°C fan for approximately 30 minutes, or until piping hot all the way through. Alternatively, reheat individual portions in the microwave for 3–5 minutes.

TIP:
You can cook the beef on the hob (2 hours low), as here, or in the oven (2 hours at 170°C fan), or in a slow cooker (6–8 hours low, 3–4 hours high).

Prep time. **30 mins**   Cook time. **2½ hours**

6. Assemble the pie: put the cooked beef into a suitable ovenproof dish and carefully spoon on the mash. Use a fork to smooth and add a swirly design if you wish. For a crispy top, lightly spray the top of the mash with olive oil. Bake in the oven for 40 minutes, until golden brown on top and cooked through.

I adore fish but I have to admit I don't cook it often enough at home. My husband isn't so keen on it and that's one reason we don't cook it, but when I made this pie he and my daughter licked their plates clean and asked for more. Make one big pie or 4 small ones, all suitable for freezing!

Fish pie

SERVES 6

FOR THE MASH
- 400g potato (e.g. Roosters), peeled and cut into cubes
- 400g sweet potatoes, peeled and cut into cubes
- 2 tablespoons butter
- 2 tablespoons milk
- a pinch of salt

FOR THE PIE
- 1 tablespoon olive oil
- 1 large carrot, peeled and finely diced
- 2 sticks of celery, finely diced
- 2 cloves of garlic, finely chopped
- 70g butter
- 70g plain flour
- 500ml warm milk
- 400g white fish, e.g. cod, hake, pollock, skinned and cut into 5cm cubes
- 200g smoked fish, e.g. coley, haddock, skinned and cut into 5cm cubes
- 1 teaspoon Dijon mustard
- 80g Cheddar cheese, grated
- salt and pepper

1. First make the mash. Bring a large pot of water to the boil, then add a pinch of salt and the regular potatoes. Cook for 8 minutes, then add the sweet potatoes and cook for a further 10–12 minutes until all the potatoes are tender. Strain and mash with the butter, milk and salt. Set aside.

2. Preheat the oven to 180°C fan. Warm a medium pan on a low heat and add the oil, then the carrot and celery and cook for 5–10 minutes until soft. Add the garlic and cook for a further minute, transfer to a heatproof bowl and set aside.

3. Add the butter to the same pan and when it has melted, quickly add the flour and mix well to a smooth paste. Cook the paste for a few minutes, then grab a whisk and slowly add the warm milk bit by bit, whisking all the time until you have a nice thick, smooth sauce. Stir in the Dijon mustard, Cheddar cheese, salt and pepper. Finally, stir in the carrot and celery, then let the sauce cool for 30 minutes.

4. To make the pie, add the fish to the sauce, gently stirring through, then pour into an ovenproof dish. Evenly distribute the mashed potato over the top, using a fork to smooth it down. Lightly spray with olive oil and bake in the oven for 40 minutes – the pie should be golden brown on top and piping hot in the centre. Serve with garden peas.

STORAGE:
Once cooked and cooled, store in an airtight container in the fridge for 3 days.

TO FREEZE:
Freeze the whole dish or divide it into portions and put it into labelled containers. Freeze for up to 3 months.

TO DEFROST:
Defrost overnight in the fridge. Reheat in the oven at 180°C fan for approximately 30 minutes, or until piping hot all the way through. Alternatively reheat individual portions in the microwave for 3–5 minutes.

TIP
If not cooking straight away, you can make the mash and creamy sauce and leave both to cool completely, then stir the diced fish through the cheesy sauce and transfer to a pie dish. Continue from step 4.

Prep time. **30 mins**   Cook time. **50 mins plus cooling time**

Chicken pie has to be the ultimate comfort food, especially on a cold winter's evening! Crispy pastry, tender chicken and sweet leeks in a creamy sauce make a mouthwatering pie!

My husband is Scottish and he says a pie should be encased in pastry, but I don't think so. I think it can be whatever you fancy, topped with mash or a pastry lid … but each to their own. Make sure to put it on the meal plan soon!

Chicken & leek pie

SERVES 6

FOR THE FILLING
- 1½ tablespoons cooking oil
- 4 chicken breasts (700g), cut into bite-size pieces
- 100g bacon bits or lardons
- 2 leeks, dark green tops removed, the rest finely sliced
- 2 sticks of celery, diced
- 2 cloves of garlic, chopped

FOR THE SAUCE
- 60g butter
- 60g plain flour
- 300ml hot chicken stock
- 300ml milk, warmed slightly
- salt and pepper
- 1 teaspoon Dijon mustard

FOR THE PASTRY LID
- 1 × 375g pack of ready-rolled puff pastry
- 1 egg and 1 tablespoon milk, whisked to make egg wash

1. Heat the oil in a large frying pan and sear the chicken until it turns white. Add the bacon bits to the pan and cook for a couple of minutes. Add the leeks, celery and garlic, stir, then reduce the heat, put a lid on the pan and cook until the vegetables are soft.

2. Meanwhile, in a separate pan, melt the butter and stir in the flour with a wooden spoon to make a paste. Cook the paste for a few minutes to cook out the flour. Measure the hot chicken stock and milk into a jug. Then, with a whisk in one hand, continually stir while slowly pouring in the liquid little by little, making sure the mixture is smooth, without lumps. Keep whisking and gradually adding the liquid until you have a smooth, thick, creamy sauce. Season with salt and pepper and stir in the mustard. If the sauce seems thin, increase the temperature and keep stirring with the whisk – it should thicken and coat the back of a wooden spoon when it's done.

3. When the sauce is ready, pour it over the chicken and vegetables and combine. Transfer to a 2-litre ovenproof dish. Loosely cover with a lid or with foil and leave the filling to cool for 1 hour.

 STORAGE:
Once cooked and cooled, store the pie in an airtight container in the fridge for up to 3 days.

 TO FREEZE:
The chicken and sauce filling can be made and frozen. To make the pie, defrost the filling in the fridge overnight and continue from step 3. Alternatively, you can freeze the whole dish or divide it between labelled containers. Freeze for up to 3 months.

 TO DEFROST:
Defrost overnight in the fridge. Reheat in the oven at 180°C fan for approximately 30 minutes, or until piping hot all the way through. Alternatively reheat individual portions in the microwave for 3–5 minutes.

Prep time. 35 mins   Cook time. 40 mins plus cooling time

4. Preheat the oven to 200°C fan. Cover the dish with the puff pastry, trimming off any extra pastry if necessary. Use a fork to seal the edges. Score the top of the pastry with a diamond design if you like, then cut an X to let steam escape and brush with the egg wash. Bake for 30 minutes, until golden on top and piping hot inside.

One reason I love pies so much is because they can be easily served family style. Just leave the cooked dishes and vegetable sides on the table and let everyone help themselves. It encourages kids to try foods for themselves without pressure. This is a delicious pie to serve up to your family.

Creamy butternut squash & mushroom filo pie

SERVES 6

1 butternut squash, peeled, deseeded and cubed, 800g
2 tablespoons olive oil
1 tablespoon paprika
1 tablespoon ground cumin
salt and pepper
1 onion, finely diced
2 cloves of garlic, chopped
1 teaspoon dried oregano
400g mushrooms, sliced
1 × 400g tin of Puy/green lentils, drained and rinsed
250g full-fat cream cheese
50g baby spinach, washed and chopped
4 sheets of filo pastry (180g)
50g butter, melted

1. Preheat the oven to 180°C fan. Put the cubed butternut squash on a baking tray and drizzle with oil. Spoon over the paprika, cumin and a pinch of salt and pepper, and toss to coat. Roast for 40–50 minutes, until soft, checking and turning the cubes a few times.

2. Whilst the squash roasts, warm a large cast-iron pot on the hob, then add a tablespoon of oil and the diced onion and cook until soft. Add the garlic, oregano and sliced mushrooms, and cook for about 10 minutes, until they brown and soften. Add a pinch of salt and pepper, and stir through the cream cheese and chopped spinach.

3. When the squash is cooked, add it to the pot, taste and adjust the seasoning if needed, then transfer to a pie dish. Leave the oven on. At this point you can chill the mix, cover it and keep it in the fridge until needed.

4. When you're ready to bake, cut the filo sheets into squares around 10cm each, brush one side with melted butter, scrunch them up and place on top of the pie. Make sure the filing is all covered with the pastry. Brush melted butter on any dry bits of pastry.

5. Bake for 30–40 minutes, until the top is golden and crispy and the filling is piping hot.

STORAGE:
Once cooked and cooled, store in an airtight container in the fridge for up to 3 days.

TO FREEZE:
The filling can be frozen for up to 3 months.

TO DEFROST:
To use the filling, defrost it overnight in the fridge, then next day transfer it to the pie dish, smooth the top and continue from step 4.

TIP:
You can swap filo pastry for ready-rolled puff pastry (a 320g pack). Just cover the dish and seal, make an X to let steam escape and brush with egg wash.

Prep time: **1 hour**   Cook time: **40 mins**

What is Italian about this pie? Well, it's the Mediterranean vegetables, the beans and the cheesy polenta. If you're not familiar with polenta you should definitely buy some and give this a go – it's really delicious. Italians focus on the quality of their ingredients and cook them simply to bring out the goodness in them.

Italian sausage polenta pie

SERVES 6

400g sausages of your choice
1 tablespoon cooking oil
1 onion, finely chopped
2 cloves of garlic, finely chopped
1 red pepper, deseeded and diced
1 medium courgette, diced
1 × 400g tin of chopped tinned tomatoes
200ml hot chicken stock
1 teaspoon dried oregano
salt and pepper
1 × 400g tin of cannellini, borlotti or butter beans, drained

FOR THE CHEESY POLENTA TOPPING
750ml hot chicken stock
120g polenta
100g grated Cheddar and mozzarella
40g finely grated Parmesan

1. Preheat the oven to 180°C and line a baking tray with baking parchment. Add the sausages and cook until nicely browned all over.

2. While the sausages are cooking, warm a large, wide pot on a medium heat. Add the oil and cook the onions for 5–10 minutes, until soft. Add the garlic, red pepper and courgette, and cook for a further few minutes. Pour in the tinned tomatoes and stock, add the oregano, season with salt and pepper and simmer for 20 minutes. Stir in the beans, then chop and add the sausages. Pour into an ovenproof dish.

3. For the polenta topping, bring the stock to the boil in a saucepan over a high heat. Reduce the heat to low and gradually add the polenta in a thin, steady stream, whisking constantly until combined. Cook, stirring, until soft, following the times given on the polenta packet. Stir in half the cheeses. Season with salt and pepper.

4. Pour the polenta over the sausage and tomato filling and scatter the remaining cheeses on top. Bake for 30 minutes, until the top is golden and the centre is piping hot.

5. Leave the pie to set for 20 minutes, then divide into portions and serve.

STORAGE:
Once cooked and cooled, store in an airtight container in the fridge for up to 3 days.

TO FREEZE:
Freeze the whole cooked dish or divide it into portions and put it into labeled containers. Freeze for up to 3 months.

TO DEFROST:
Defrost overnight in the fridge. Reheat in the oven at 180°C fan for approximately 30 minutes, or until piping hot all the way through. Alternatively reheat individual portions in the microwave for 3-5 minutes.

Prep time. **35 mins**   Cook time. **30 mins plus cooling**

What is bobotie? It's a South African dish made with sweet curried lamb, raisins and a savoury yellow custard lid. It's traditionally served with rice cooked with turmeric so it turns yellow. A fruit chutney made with banana and mango is also popular, and a coconut relish or fresh coconut can also accompany the dish. Bobotie was one of the first dishes the head chef asked me to make when I worked at The Kitchen in Galway. In my house, we are not used to adding sweet dried fruit to meat dishes, but this is delicious and always gets the conversation going at dinner time about different food cultures.

Bobotie

SERVES 4

- 1 slice of white bread, crusts removed
- 250ml milk
- 450g lamb or beef mince
- 2 tablespoons cooking oil
- 1 onion, finely diced
- 2 cloves of garlic, finely chopped
- 1 tablespoon curry powder
- 1 tablespoon apricot jam or mango chutney
- 1 tablespoon Worcestershire sauce
- 2 teaspoons ground turmeric
- 1 tablespoon cider vinegar or lemon juice
- salt and black pepper
- 50g raisins
- 2 large eggs
- 2 bay leaves

1. Preheat the oven to 180°C fan. Put the bread and milk into a bowl and leave to soak for 1 minute, then squeeze most of the milk out and put it on a plate, saving the milk for later.

2. Heat a large pan and brown the mince until no pink remains, then drain through a sieve and discard the fat. Set the browned mince aside.

3. In the same pan heat the oil and fry the onions until softened. Then add the garlic, curry powder, jam and Worcestershire sauce, 1 teaspoon of turmeric, vinegar and salt and pepper. Mix together and cook for a few minutes.

4. Next add the soaked bread and the raisins, and put the lamb back into the pan. Cook over a low heat for a few minutes, then transfer to a pie dish and smooth the top with the back of a spoon.

5. To make the custard, crack 2 eggs into the saved milk, add another teaspoon of turmeric and salt, and whisk well. Pour over the meat mixture and place the bay leaf on top. Bake uncovered for approximately 1 hour, or until set and nicely browned.

STORAGE:
Once cooked and cooled, store in an airtight container in the fridge for up to 3 days.

TO FREEZE:
Freeze the whole cooked dish or divide it into portions and put it into labeled containers. Freeze for up to 3 months.

TO DEFROST:
Defrost overnight in the fridge. Reheat in the oven at 180°C fan for approximately 30 minutes, or until piping hot all the way through. Alternatively reheat individual portions in the microwave for 3–5 minutes.

Prep time. **20 mins**   Cook time. **1 hour**

Family Pies & Delicious Dishes

I had to have a lasagne in my book. I think it's such a clever dish, with delicious layers of flavour. And the best part is it always tastes better the next day. Sweet potato and spinach are my healthy veggie twist. Serve it family-style with garlic bread and salad.

Sweet potato, feta & spinach lasagne

SERVES 6

FOR THE SWEET POTATO FILLING

- 4 small sweet potatoes (800g), peeled and cut into 2cm cubes
- 1 tablespoon paprika
- 1 tablespoon ground cumin
- 4 tablespoons cooking oil
- 200g baby spinach, washed and chopped

FOR THE QUICK TOMATO SAUCE

- 2 × 400g tins of chopped tomatoes
- 2 tablespoons tomato purée
- 2 cloves of garlic, crushed
- 2 teaspoons honey or sugar
- 2 teaspoons dried oregano
- 1 teaspoon salt

FOR THE WHITE SAUCE

- 60g butter
- 60g plain flour
- 600ml milk, warmed slightly
- a pinch of nutmeg
- 50g grated Cheddar and mozzarella

TO ASSEMBLE THE LASAGNE

- 150g feta, crumbled
- 6–8 sheets of lasagne
- 150g grated Cheddar and mozzarella

1. For the sweet potato filling, preheat the oven to 180°C fan and line two baking trays with baking parchment. Put the sweet potato cubes into a mixing bowl, spoon over the paprika and cumin, drizzle with oil, and divide between the baking trays. Roast in the oven for 20 minutes, or until the sweet potatoes are soft and golden.

2. For the quick tomato sauce, put all the ingredients into a large pan, then pour a bit of water into the tomato tins to rinse them out and add this to the pan too. Stir to combine, bring to the boil, then turn down to a simmer for 20 minutes.

3. For the white sauce, melt the butter in a saucepan, then add the flour, stirring to form a smooth paste. Cook on a low heat, stirring for a few minutes to cook out the flour. Swap the wooden spoon for a whisk, then pour in a little warm milk and whisk well to avoid lumps. Slowly add the rest of the milk a little at a time, whisking continuously until the sauce thickens – this will take a few minutes. Grate in the nutmeg and add 50g of grated cheese and a pinch of salt and pepper.

4. To assemble the lasagne, mix the tomato sauce with the roasted sweet potato and the chopped spinach. Take a large

STORAGE:
Once cooked and cooled, store in an airtight container in the fridge for up to 3 days.

TO FREEZE:
It's best to freeze the whole dish, or you can divide it into portions and put it into labelled containers. Freeze for up to 3 months.

TO DEFROST:
Defrost overnight in the fridge. Reheat in the oven at 180°C fan for approximately 30 minutes, or until piping hot all the way through. Alternatively reheat individual portions in the microwave for 3–5 minutes.

Recipe continued on page 161

 Prep time. **35 mins**   Cook time. **40mins**

lasagne dish and put half the sweet potato and tomato mix into the bottom, sprinkle on half the feta, smoothing to form an even layer. Place 3 or 4 lasagne sheets on top, then pour on half the white sauce and smooth it out. Add the rest of the sweet potato mix, top with the rest of the feta, add another 3 or 4 lasagne sheets, then pour the rest of the white sauce over the top and scatter over the rest of the grated cheese.

5. Cover the dish with foil and cook in the oven for 40 minutes. Remove and bake without the foil for a further 20 minutes. It should be bubbling and golden, and cooked through.

6. Leave the lasagne to set for 30 minutes, then serve with garlic bread and salad.

This is a real budget-friendly meal and can be made with mostly store-cupboard ingredients! I like to make a quick tomato sauce to add lots of flavour to the bean filling. The tortilla wraps are then filled and bathed in the sauce, topped with cheese and oven baked.

Red pepper & black bean enchiladas

SERVES 4-6

FOR THE SAUCE
- 2 × 400g tins of chopped tomatoes
- 2 tablespoons tomato purée
- 2 cloves of garlic, finely chopped
- 2 teaspoons honey
- 2 teaspoons paprika
- 1 teaspoon ground cumin
- 1 teaspoon ground coriander
- 1 teaspoon dried oregano
- 1 teaspoon salt

FOR THE FILLING
- 1 tablespoon cooking oil
- 1 onion, finely diced
- 1 red pepper, deseeded and finely diced
- salt and pepper
- 2 × 400g tins of black beans, rinsed and drained
- 2 teaspoons chilli sauce, optional
- a bunch of fresh coriander, finely chopped (30g)
- 200g feta cheese, crumbled

FOR THE REST
- 6-8 large tortilla wraps
- 100g Cheddar cheese, grated

TO SERVE
- sour cream
- lime quarters
- jalapeños, if you like more spice

1. To make the sauce, put all the ingredients into a pan, then add a bit of water to the tomato tins to rinse them out and pour this into the pan too. Bring to the boil, then reduce the heat and simmer uncovered for 20 minutes, until the sauce has reduced and thickened.

2. For the filling, heat a wide frying pan, then add the oil, onion and red pepper and cook until soft. Sprinkle in a small pinch of salt and pepper. Add the black beans, and the chilli sauce (if using), and mash the beans a bit with a fork. Add a ladle of the tomato sauce, then transfer to a bowl to cool for 10 minutes. Then stir through half the fresh coriander and half the crumbled feta.

3. Preheat the oven to 180°C fan. To assemble, pour one-third of the tomato sauce on to the bottom of an ovenproof dish. Take the tortilla wraps and add a couple of tablespoons of the filling to each one, then roll them to make a cigar shape and line them neatly in the dish – depending on the size of the dish you may fit in 6–8. Pour the rest of the sauce over the top then scatter over the Cheddar cheese and the rest of the feta.

4. Bake in the oven for 30 minutes, until bubbly and golden on top.

STORAGE:
Once cooked and cooled, store in an airtight container in the fridge for up to 3 days.

FREEZER:
It's best to freeze the whole dish or divide it into portions and put it into labelled containers. Freeze for up to 3 months.

TO DEFROST:
Defrost overnight in the fridge. Reheat in the oven at 180°C fan for approximately 30 minutes, or until piping hot all the way through. Alternatively reheat individual portions in the microwave for 3–5 minutes.

Prep time. **35 mins**   Cook time. **30 mins**

If your kids love pizza and pasta they will love this! My husband makes a mean macaroni cheese, and I threw him a curve ball when I suggested adding some pizza flavours to this one! I've topped it with pasta sauce, cheese and pepperoni. Make it your new family favourite

Pizza macaroni cheese

SERVES 6

FOR THE SAUCE
- 1½ tablespoons olive oil
- 1 onion, finely diced
- 1 red pepper, deseeded and finely diced
- 2 cloves of garlic, finely chopped
- 5 slices of pepperoni, chopped
- 800ml milk, warmed slightly
- 70g plain flour
- 70g butter
- salt and pepper
- 100g Cheddar cheese and mozzarella, grated

FOR THE REST
- 300g dried macaroni, or similar small pasta shape
- 200ml tomato sauce, shop-bought or home-made (for homemade, see Lasagne recipe, page 158)
- 100g Cheddar cheese and mozzarella, grated
- 5 pepperoni slices, cut in half

1. Preheat the oven to 180°C fan and cook the pasta according to the packet instructions.
2. Warm a large pan over a medium heat, add the oil and the onions and cook for 5 minutes without browning the onions. Add the diced peppers and garlic, plus a pinch of salt, and cook until soft. Stir through the chopped pepperoni and cook for a few minutes more, then transfer to a plate and set to one side.
3. Pour the warm milk into a jug. Using the same large pan in which you cooked the onion mix, add the butter and let it melt, then add the flour, stir with a wooden spoon to make a paste, and cook for a few minutes. Slowly pour the warm milk into the pot while whisking until all the milk is in the pot. Cook and stir until the sauce thickens – this can take 5–10 minutes. Add a pinch of salt and pepper, then stir in the cheese.
4. Add the cooked and drained pasta and the cooked onion mix to the white sauce and stir well to combine, tasting and adjusting the seasoning if needed. Transfer the mix to an ovenproof dish. Top evenly with the sauce, the remaining cheese and finally the pepperoni slices.
5. Carefully place the dish in a preheated oven and bake until the cheese is browned and bubbly, approximately 15–20 minutes. Allow the pasta to cool slightly before serving.

STORAGE:
Once cooked and cooled, store in an airtight container in the fridge for up to 3 days.

TO FREEZE:
It's best to freeze the whole dish or divide it into portions and put it into labelled containers. Freeze for up to 3 months.

TO DEFROST:
Defrost overnight in the fridge. Reheat in the oven at 180°C fan for approximately 30 minutes, or until piping hot all the way through. Alternatively reheat individual portions in the microwave for 3–5 minutes.

Prep time. 30 mins   Cook time. 20 mins

If you're keen to introduce more pulses and veggies to the weekly menu, this is one to try. It's a clever mix of veggies and lentils with familiar curry flavours.

I had a friend over for dinner and I cooked her this dish. She absolutely loved it and asked what meat I'd used, to which I replied, 'None!' Lentils and mushrooms make a great alternative to meat. Just wait until you serve up this pie – everyone will be dying to dive right in.

Curry lentil pie

SERVES 6

FOR THE MASH
- 800g potatoes, peeled and chopped into 2cm cubes
- ½ a head of cauliflower, cut into florets
- 100g butter, melted
- 1 tablespoon curry powder

FOR THE FILLING
- 1½ tablespoons cooking oil
- 1 onion, finely diced
- 2 cloves of garlic, finely chopped or grated
- 2 tablespoons tomato purée
- 3 tablespoons curry powder
- salt and pepper, to taste
- 250g mushrooms, cut into small dice
- 2 cooked beetroots, cut into small dice
- 2 × 400g tins of Puy lentils, drained
- 450g hot vegetable stock

1. For the mash bring a pan of water to the boil, and add some salt and the potato cubes. Cook for 10 minutes, then add the cauliflower florets and cook for a further 5–8 minutes.

2. For the filling, heat a wide pot on the hob. Add the oil and the diced onions, and sauté on a low heat for 5–10 minutes, or until the onions are soft. Stir in the garlic, tomato purée, curry powder, salt and pepper, and cook for 2 minutes to toast the spices. Next, add the chopped mushrooms, stirring to coat them in the curry mixture, and cook for another 5 minutes until softened. Finally, add the chopped cooked beetroot, drained Puy lentils, and stock. Stir well and let it simmer for 30 minutes.

3. Mash the cooked potatoes and cauliflower together with the melted butter, a pinch of salt, and the tablespoon of curry powder.

4. Taste and adjust the seasoning as needed. Transfer the curry lentil mixture to a suitable ovenproof dish, top with the mash, and bake in the oven for 30 minutes. Alternatively, you can place it under a hot grill for 5–10 minutes, until the top is golden and crispy.

STORAGE:
Once cooked and cooled, store in an airtight container in the fridge for 3 days.

TO FREEZE:
It's best to freeze the whole dish or divide it into portions and put it into labelled containers. Freeze for up to 3 months.

TO DEFROST:
Defrost overnight in the fridge. Reheat in the oven at 180°C fan for approximately 30 minutes, or until piping hot all the way through. Alternatively reheat individual portions in the microwave for 3–5 minutes.

Prep time. **40 mins**   Cook time. **30 mins**

Chapter 8

Better-than-Shop-bought Treats

The shops are full of overpriced treats made with a long list of ingredients including additives and preservatives. These delicious, super-easy, no-bake bars were a viral hit for me and are way less processed than the shop-bought ones. I hope you love them and make them on repeat!

Crunch bars

MAKES 12

200g chocolate (milk or dark)
40g coconut oil
200g peanut butter (I use smooth)
100g puffed rice

1. Line a 20cm square baking tin with baking parchment. Melt the chocolate and coconut oil together in the microwave or in a bowl over a pot of simmering water. Stir in the peanut butter until it's all nice and smooth.

2. Gently stir in the puffed rice, then pour the mix into the baking tin. Set in the fridge for at least 2 hours, then slice into bars or squares.

STORAGE:
Store in an airtight container in the fridge for up to 3 days.

TO FREEZE:
Place the bars in a labelled ziplock bag. Freeze for up to 3 months.

TO DEFROST:
Defrost overnight in the fridge.

TIP:
These bars are best kept in the fridge, as they can melt easily on sunny days.

Prep time. **10 mins**   Chill time. **2 hours**

There's nothing nicer than a homemade biscuit. Gingernuts are a classic and my kids love these gently spiced biscuits too. While it's easy to pick up a packet, I bet you'll prefer this homemade version, especially with a big glass of cold milk.

Gingernut biscuits

MAKES 16 SMALL

100g plain flour
1 flat teaspoon baking powder
½ teaspoon bicarbonate of soda
1½ teaspoons ground ginger

30g caster sugar
50g butter, melted
2 tablespoons golden syrup

1. Preheat the oven to 170°C fan and line two baking trays with baking parchment. Sieve the flour, baking powder, bicarbonate of soda and ginger into a mixing bowl, then stir in the sugar.
2. Melt the butter in the microwave and stir in the golden syrup. Pour into the bowl of flour and stir until the mixture comes together to form a soft dough. Divide the dough into 2 pieces, then divide each of those into 8 and roll between the palms of your hands until you have 16 equal balls. Put the balls on the baking trays, spaced apart, and gently push down to flatten with the palm of your hand.
3. Bake for 10–12 minutes, until golden and cracked on top. Leave to firm up on the trays for 10 minutes, then transfer to a wire rack to cool completely.

STORAGE:
Store in an airtight container for up to 1 week.

TO FREEZE:
Leave to cool completely, then place on a tray lined with baking parchment and freeze flat. Pack into a labelled freezer bag or container and return to the freezer. Freeze for up to 3 months.

TO DEFROST:
Leave to defrost at room temperature before serving.

TIP:
The trick is to not over-mix the dough or over-bake the biscuits.

Prep time. **15 mins**   Cook time. **12 mins plus cooling time**

One of my favourite things to do is to come up with no-bake snack recipes that are healthier than shop-bought and taste delicious as a treat. These bars are similar to a well-known biscuit bar, but healthier. I'll always make these on a Friday for the kids coming in from school. I often use different nut butters so they have a different flavour. The caramel can be used for lots of things: serve it with pancakes, layer on top of brownies or eat with breadsticks as a dip it's so delicious!

No-bake caramel bars

MAKES 8 BARS

FOR THE CARAMEL
200g pitted dates, chopped
2 tablespoons coconut oil
1 tablespoon nut butter, e.g. peanut, almond, cashew
4 tablespoons maple syrup or honey
3–4 tablespoons boiling water

FOR THE BASE
100g oats
15g cocoa powder
30g coconut oil
2 tablespoons boiling water

FOR THE TOP
80g milk chocolate
20g coconut oil

1. Line a loaf tin with baking parchment (a similar-sized lunchbox will work too).
2. Put all the caramel ingredients into a powerful blender and blend until smooth. Take out three-quarters of the caramel, put it into a bowl and set to one side.
3. Add the oats, cocoa powder, coconut oil and boiling water to the caramel left in the blender, and blend until combined.
4. Spoon the base mix into the loaf tin and smooth level with a spoon or spatula. Top with the caramel and smooth flat. Put into the fridge for 1 hour to set.
5. Melt the chocolate and coconut oil together. Pour over the top of the caramel and tilt the tin to cover. Chill for 30 minutes. Slice into bars and enjoy.

STORAGE:
Keep in the fridge for up to 5 days.

 TO FREEZE:
Freeze in labelled ziplock bags for up to 3 months.

 TO DEFROST:
Defrost in a container overnight.

Prep time. **20 mins**   Chill time. **30 mins**

These cookies are very special in my house. I've been baking them with my daughter Meabh since she started school at five years old. We would bake them after school on a Friday, and sit and chat afterwards about the week and what we'd do for the weekend. Spending this time baking with my kids is so precious – we are making memories. Meabh named these herself on one of those very afternoons.

Meabh's memory cookies

MAKES APPROX. 18

90g butter, softened
80g soft light brown sugar
3 large eggs
3 tablespoons honey
1 teaspoon vanilla extract

300g porridge oats
2 teaspoons baking powder
100g chocolate chips, plus 20g to finish

1. Preheat the oven to 180°C fan, and line two baking trays with baking parchment.

2. Cube the butter and place in a mixing bowl with the sugar, then use a wooden spoon to mix until creamy. Whisk the eggs in a separate small bowl, then pour into the mixing bowl. Add the honey and vanilla and mix again – if it's very lumpy, use a whisk to break up the lumps. Add the oats and baking powder, mix well, then fold in the chocolate chips.

3. Scoop the cookies on to the baking trays, using about a heaped tablespoon for each, leaving a gap between them. If you have a cookie cutter, use it to make the cookies round and push down the cookie dough with the back of a small spoon. If you don't have a cookie cutter, just push down with a spoon and try to keep the shape as round as possible. Top with the remaining chocolate chips.

4. Bake the cookies for 12–15 minutes, until golden brown. Leave to cool for 20 minutes, then tuck in.

STORAGE:
Cool completely, then store in an airtight container for up to 3 days.

TO FREEZE:
Lay flat in labelled ziplock bags and freeze for up to 3 months.

TO DEFROST:
Defrost as many cookies as you wish in an airtight container on the worktop overnight.

Prep time. **15 mins**   Cook time. **15 mins**

This is such a quick treat to put together and great fun to eat. I've made it so many times for my kids, especially in the summer months – it's a great one for play dates on sunny days. The best fun is cracking it into shards to share.

Frozen yoghurt bark

SERVES 4

500g vanilla-flavoured yoghurt
150g fresh berries, e.g. strawberries, raspberries, blueberries

30g chopped nuts, e.g. hazelnuts, pistachios (optional)

1. Line a large baking tray with baking parchment and spread the yoghurt over the parchment in an even layer.
2. Scatter your chosen toppings (fruits, nuts) evenly over the yoghurt. Freeze for 2 hours or until solid.
3. Carefully peel away the paper, then break the yoghurt into shards and place in a freezer bag.

TO FREEZE:
Freeze in labelled ziplock bags for for up to 3 months. Serve on plates, straight from the freezer.

Prep time. **10 mins**   Freezing time. **2 hours**

Better-Than-Shop-bought Treats

These donuts are so cute to make at home and so much healthier than classic deep-fried donuts! My kids were always begging me for shop-bought donuts, but they have told me they now prefer these ones. For easy decorating, just dip them in chocolate and top with sprinkles.

Easy donuts

MAKES 12–16, DEPENDING ON THE SIZE OF YOUR MOULDS

150g butter, softened
100g caster sugar
1 large egg
175g plain flour
1 teaspoon baking powder
100ml whole milk
1 teaspoon vanilla extract

TOPPINGS
100g dark/milk/white chocolate, melted
sprinkles

1. Preheat the oven to 170°C fan. Lightly grease your donut tin. Measure the butter and sugar into a mixing bowl and beat with a wooden spoon or an electric mixer until light and fluffy. This will take a few minutes.
2. Crack in the egg and beat well.
3. Sieve the flour and baking powder into a separate bowl and mix well. Measure the milk into a jug and stir in the vanilla extract.
4. Pour half the milk into the flour mix, then beat until smooth.
5. Pour in the other half of the milk, but don't beat this time. Just stir to combine.
6. To make the next part easy, use a piping bag or food-safe bag to pipe the batter into the donut moulds. If using a food-safe bag, add the batter and snip off a corner. Don't overfill the donut moulds, leave room for them to rise. Bake for 12–18 minutes, depending on the size of the donuts, using a cocktail stick to check they're done. Cool completely.
7. To decorate, melt the chocolate in a bowl in the microwave, dip the donut in the chocolate, then top with sprinkles.

TO FREEZE:
Freeze the plain or decorated donuts in a labelled ziplock bag for up to 3 months.

TO DEFROST:
Defrost overnight in an airtight container on the worktop.

TIP:
Donut tins can vary in size. If you don't have a donut tin, just make regular cupcakes instead.

Prep time. **15 mins** Cook time. **28 mins plus decorating time**

Rocky roads are great fun to make – just crush and add your favourite biscuits, marshmallows and chocolate sweets! We used to make them in the café I worked in, and my boss would add pink squares of Cadbury's Turkish delight – a rose-flavoured jelly covered in chocolate. I'm not a fan of Turkish delight, but feel free to add some if you are.

This is most definitely an indulgent treat. It's great for an occasion or a celebration such as a birthday party. At Hallowe'en, for a festive twist, add some mint and orange Aero. At Christmas add some red and green M&Ms.

Rocky road

MAKES 12 SQUARES

300g milk chocolate
4 tablespoons golden syrup
100g butter (I use salted)
100g mini marshmallows
150g rich tea biscuits or digestives, broken into small pieces

OPTIONAL ADD-INS (100g)

nuts, e.g. walnuts, pecans, hazelnuts
dried fruit, e.g. cranberries, raisins, dates
honeycomb or Crunchie bar

1. Line a 20cm square tin with baking parchment.
2. Melt the chocolate, golden syrup and butter together in a bowl in the microwave or in a pan on a very low heat, then set aside to cool for 10 minutes.
3. Add the marshmallows, biscuits and chopped Crunchie bars and stir to combine. Pour into the tin and gently press down.
4. Set in the fridge for 2 hours at least (overnight is best), then divide into squares.

STORAGE:
The squares can be stored in an airtight container for up to 5 days.

TO FREEZE:
Freeze the squares in a labelled ziplock bag for up to 3 months.

TO DEFROST:
Defrost overnight in an airtight container on the worktop.

Prep time. **15 mins**   Chill time. **2 hours**

In most supermarkets you can buy mini cupcakes in a plastic container – the vanilla and chocolate chip ones are always popular. If you check the ingredient list, however, it's always very long, with lots of additives and preservatives. The great news is that these have just six recognizable ingredients! If you make your own you know exactly what you're eating, and that's always a bonus in my mind.

We love these for picnics on a summer's day or as a treat at the weekend. Mini ones are especially great because they go a little bit further!

Mini vanilla cupcakes

MAKES 24–30

115g butter, softened
90g caster sugar
2 eggs
1 teaspoon vanilla extract
115g self-raising flour
1–2 tablespoons milk

1. Preheat the oven to 170°C fan. Line a 24-hole mini muffin tin with paper cases. In a mixing bowl, combine the butter and sugar, and beat with an electric mixer or a wooden spoon until the mixture is light and fluffy. In a jug, mix the eggs and vanilla, then gradually incorporate them into the butter mixture.

2. Sift the flour into the mixture, adding a little milk as you go, and gently mix in by hand until no traces of flour remain. The batter should be loose enough to easily fall from a spoon. Divide the batter between the cases.

3. Bake the cupcakes for 10–12 minutes, or until they are slightly golden brown. Allow them to cool in the tin for 5 minutes, then gently lift them out to cool completely on a wire rack.

STORAGE:
Cool completely and store in an airtight container for up to 3 days.

TO FREEZE:
Freeze the cooled vanilla muffins in a labelled ziplock bag for up to 3 months.

TO DEFROST:
Defrost overnight in an airtight container on the worktop.

TIP:
This recipe can also be used to make 12 regular cupcakes – bake them for 20–22 minutes.

Breakfast cereal is a great ingredient for homemade snacks. I love using cornflakes, hoops and puffed rice.

Yes, you can buy rice cereal treats, but it is so incredibly easy to make your own version. I love a no-bake recipe, and these are super easy to make and only three ingredients. Perfect for birthday parties!

No-bake bubble rice treats

MAKES 12 SQUARES

180g puffed rice cereal
120g coconut oil
150g white chocolate

1. Line a 20cm square baking tin with baking parchment.
2. Measure the puffed rice into a mixing bowl. Melt the coconut oil and white chocolate together in the microwave, checking and stirring frequently to prevent the chocolate from burning, or use a heatproof bowl over a pan of simmering water.
3. Pour the chocolate mix over the puffed rice and stir to coat. Transfer to the prepared baking tin and smooth the top, using a square piece of parchment paper to press down to compact the mix.
4. Chill for at least 2 hours, then cut into squares using a large carving knife.

STORAGE:
The squares can be kept in an airtight container for up to 3 days.

TO FREEZE:
Freeze the squares in a labelled ziplock bag for up to 3 months.

TO DEFROST:
Defrost overnight in an airtight container on the worktop.

Prep time. **15 mins**   Chill time. **2 hours**

Whoever invented the brownie was a genius. I've baked brownies for years and I never tire of making them. These are great to bring on a visit to a friend's house or to bake and pop candles in as a birthday cake.

If we are ever out for the day shopping and stop off at a café, one of us will usually order a brownie. It is always a treat, but so much nicer if you make it yourself.

Double chocolate brownies

MAKES 16

200g milk chocolate
200g butter
3 eggs
200g caster sugar
1 teaspoon vanilla extract

115g plain flour
30g cocoa powder
200g milk or dark chocolate, chopped into chunks

1. Preheat the oven to 180°C fan, and line a 23cm square tray with baking parchment. Melt the chocolate and butter together in the microwave, or in a pan on a low heat, stir and set aside to cool for 5 minutes.

2. In a separate bowl, whisk the eggs and sugar together, using a hand whisk or an electric whisk, until the mixture turns a pale yellow, then add the vanilla. Then pour in the melted chocolate and butter mix, stir gently to combine.

3. Sieve in the plain flour and cocoa powder, then stir, using a rubber spatula. Add the chocolate chunks.

4. Pour the mix into the prepared tin, tilting the tin to get the mix into the corners and smoothing the top with the back of a spoon. Bake for approximately 25 minutes. Check that it's cooked to your liking by inserting a knife or a cocktail stick – it should be slightly gooey, but will set when it cools.

5. Cut into squares and enjoy with fresh whipped cream or ice cream.

STORAGE:
The squares can be stored in an airtight container for up to 3 days.

TO FREEZE:
Freeze the brownie squares in a labelled ziplock bag for up to 3 months.

TO DEFROST:
Defrost overnight in an airtight container on the worktop.

TIP:
To change things up, try adding nuts, such as flaked almonds, walnuts, pecans, or dried fruit like raisins, cranberries, chopped dates.

Prep time. **20 mins**   Cook time. **30 mins**

Chapter 9

Bread

This bread sure is a miracle. It's so easy to make, but just needs some time overnight to work its magic. I like to measure it out on a Saturday evening and bake it fresh on Sunday morning to have for lunch that day. The bread is really nice to slice and dip into homemade soup – or stash some slices in the freezer to defrost for Gypsy Bread – see the Breakfast section (page 34). I often send thick slices to school with a flask of soup for lunch.

Miracle loaf (no-knead)

MAKES 1 LOAF

500g strong bread flour
1 × 7g sachet of dried yeast

2 teaspoons fine salt
330ml lukewarm water

1. Measure the flour, yeast and salt into a large mixing bowl, and stir well. Pour in the water little by little and mix with a wooden spoon to form a shaggy dough. Flour your hands and bring the dough together to form a ball in the bowl. Cover with cling film or a damp tea towel and leave the bowl in an ambient spot in the kitchen overnight, 12–13 hours.

2. Next day, flour the worktop and gently scoop the dough out of the bowl. Be gentle with it, don't knock out all the air. Bring the dough into a round shape and sprinkle some flour on top. Place on a floured piece of baking parchment. Cover with a damp tea towel and leave to rise for 1 hour in a warm place.

3. 20 minutes into the dough-rising time, preheat the oven to 230°C fan. Place a 24cm cast-iron pot with a lid (or similar) in the oven for 30 minutes to heat up. After this time, take the hot pot from the oven. Carefully lift the paper and dough and put it into the pot, then slash the top of the dough with a sharp knife and add any design you wish. Pour 2 tablespoons of water into the pot and replace the lid. Bake for 30 minutes, then take the lid off and bake for a further 10–15 minutes, until nicely golden on top.

4. Place the bread on a wire rack to cool for 30 minutes, then slice and enjoy.

STORAGE:
Store in an airtight container in the cupboard for up to 3 days.

TO FREEZE:
The loaf can be frozen whole or in slices. Place in a labelled ziplock bag and freeze for up to 3 months.

TO DEFROST:
Defrost overnight in an airtight container, ready to use in the morning.

Prep time. 10 mins   Cook time. 45 mins plus overnight prove

Who doesn't love pizza? It is the most requested food in our house! I sometimes think my kids are part Italian, with their love of pasta and pizza.

I've been making pizza dough with my kids since they were very small. We always make a batch so we can freeze half the dough balls for the next pizza night, which is usually the next Friday night. There is flour everywhere and bits of dough get walked into the floor, but it's always worth it to have the most delicious homemade, wonky-shaped pizzas.

Pizza dough & homemade pizza

MAKES 8 DOUGH BALLS (FREEZE 4/COOK 4)

630ml tepid water (mix 200ml boiling water with 430ml cold water)
2 × 7g sachets of dried yeast
2 tablespoons olive oil
2 teaspoons sugar
1kg flour (use bread flour or strong flour)
2 teaspoons salt

1. To make the pizza dough, add the yeast, oil and sugar to the tepid water, stir and set aside for 15 minutes.
2. Measure the flour and salt into a bowl or a standing mixer. Pour in the yeast mixture. Stir and knead the dough in the mixer or by hand. Knead it for at least 10 minutes.
3. Once kneaded, take the dough out of the bowl, then lightly oil the bowl, put the dough back in and cover with a tea towel. Leave the bowl and dough in a warm spot in your kitchen for 1½ hours, or until doubled in size.
4. Punch the air out of the dough, then flour a worktop and divide the dough into 8 even pieces, approximately 190g each. Roll them into smooth round balls. Dust two trays with flour and set 4 balls on each. Cover with a clean tea towel or cling film and leave to prove once more for about 30 minutes.

TO FREEZE THE DOUGH:
If the tray fits the 4 dough balls, cover with cling film or tin foil and put it straight into the freezer. After 3 hours, use a spatula to prise the dough off the tray, place in small food bags and return them to the freezer. They will keep for 3 months.

TO DEFROST:
Take the dough balls from the freezer and place them on a floured tray. Cover with cling film and defrost in the fridge overnight. The next day, take them from the fridge and leave for an hour or two to reach room temperature. Then dust the worktop with flour and make your pizza as on page 198.

Recipe continued on page 198

TO MAKE THE PIZZA

Preheat the oven to 200°C fan. Dust the worktop with flour, then, using your hands, gently push out the dough ball, keeping the round shape, aiming for 23cm wide. Stretch it if needed. Transfer to a baking tray, top with pizza sauce, cheese and the toppings of your choice, adding the toppings sparingly. Cook for 10–12 minutes. To cook the base of the pizza, remove the tray and cook the pizza on the bars of the oven for the last 2 minutes of the cooking time.

 STORAGE:
The cooked pizza slices will keep in an airtight container in the fridge for up to 3 days.

 TO FREEZE:
Freeze cooked pizza slices in labelled ziplock bags for up to 3 months.

 TO DEFROST:
Defrost in an airtight container in the fridge overnight. Reheat in the oven preheated to 180°C fan for 10 minutes, or until piping hot.

I've made focaccia many times and have always found the overnight fridge version works best. Leaving the flour and yeast to prove slowly in the fridge gives a better flavour and allows it to develop air bubbles. This bread loves olive oil, so be generous. It makes a great sandwich bread for an epic lunch or a marvellous picnic.

Overnight 'fridge' focaccia

MAKES 1 LOAF

1 × 7g sachet of dried yeast
430ml lukewarm water (mix 130ml boiling water with 300ml cold water – it should be body temperature, 36°C)

500g strong flour/bread flour
2 teaspoons salt
olive oil
sea salt

1. To a jug add the dried yeast to the lukewarm water and let it sit for 15 minutes, then stir.
2. Measure the flour and salt into a large mixing bowl and stir to combine. Pour in the yeast and water, and mix with a wooden spoon to form a sticky ball. Use 1 tablespoon of oil to coat a second mixing bowl and transfer the dough into it. Using your hand, lightly oil the top of the dough. Cover the bowl with a lid, cling film or a damp tea towel to make it airtight, and put the bowl into the fridge for at least 12 hours (ideally overnight).
3. Line a 23cm x 33cm baking tin – I recommend using baking parchment. Now oil the baking tin with 2 tablespoons of olive oil.
4. Oil your hands, then scoop the dough out of the bowl and straight on to the baking tray. Rub the oil all over the dough, and smooth and push it into the corners of the baking tray. Cover the tray with a clean plastic bag, or cling film, and let the dough rest for 3–4 hours to warm up and double in size.
5. Preheat the oven to 220°C fan. Pour the remaining 1 tablespoon of olive oil over the dough and rub lightly with your hands, then using your fingers press straight down to create deep dimples. Sprinkle generously with sea salt all over.
6. Bake for 25–30 minutes, until cooked and the bottom is golden brown. Transfer to a rack. Cool for 10 minutes before cutting and serving.

STORAGE:
The focaccia will keep in an airtight box for up to 3 days.

TO FREEZE:
Freeze in a large labelled ziplock bag for up to 3 months.

TO DEFROST:
Defrost in an airtight container on the worktop overnight.

TIP:
This focaccia makes amazing sandwiches. Cut and slice a square in half and fill with your favourite sandwich fillings like lettuce, hummus and roast veggies or sliced meat. Delicious as a packed lunch or picnic.

Prep time. **15 mins**   Cook time. **30 mins plus overnight prove**

Sometimes only a super-soft bread roll will do. If I was to make bread every single day it would be this bread. It takes a bit of effort, but it is so worth it. It's based on a Japanese milk bread — the tangzhong is a cooked paste that gets added to the rest of the ingredients and makes the softest, fluffiest rolls.

Super-soft bread rolls

MAKES 16 SMALL ROLLS

FOR THE BREAD DOUGH

550g strong bread flour (bread flour is needed for its high protein levels)
10g fast-acting dried yeast
30g granulated sugar
5g fine salt
100g salted butter, at room temperature, cut into cubes
extra flour for dusting

FOR THE TANGZHONG

50g strong bread flour
200ml whole milk, plus
260ml whole milk (cold) to be added later

1. Put the bread flour, yeast, sugar and salt into a mixing bowl, and mix well to combine.

2. To make the tangzhong, put the flour and 200ml milk into a small pan. Gently heat and whisk continually until you have a thick, gloopy paste. Don't walk away from the pan during this time. Once it's smooth and gloopy, take the pot off the heat and whisk in the 260ml cold milk. The temperature of the milk needs to be 36°C or body temperature – check with a thermometer or with your finger.

3. Pour the milk mixture into the mixing bowl. If using a mixer, attach the dough hook and knead for a few minutes until the dough starts coming together, or do this step by hand. When it looks like a rough shaggy dough, cover with a tea towel and let it rest for 5 minutes. After this time, run the mixer and add the butter a piece at a time, kneading for a good 10–15 minutes until the dough is nice and soft. If kneading by hand, just add a few cubes of butter at a time and knead until incorporated. Take the dough out of the bowl, shape it into a round ball and put it back into the bowl, cover with a clean tea towel and leave to prove in a warm place for about 1 hour, or until doubled in size. It may take longer if your kitchen is cold.

STORAGE:
Once cool, store the rolls in an airtight container in the cupboard for up to 3 days.

TO FREEZE:
Freeze in labelled ziplock bags for up to 3 months.

TO DEFROST:
Defrost overnight in an airtight container, ready to use for school lunches in the morning.

TIP:
I make the dough in a standing mixer, but it can be made by hand.

Recipe continued on page 204

Prep time. 30 mins   Cook time. 25 mins plus prove time

4. Oil a large 33cm baking tray, or two smaller trays. Knock the air out of the dough and divide it into 16 even balls about 70g each. Roll into smooth round balls as best you can, using your hands. Cover with a tea towel and leave for 10 minutes, then roll again to tighten them. Place on the tray, spaced 2–3cm apart. Cover with a clean tea towel and leave to double in size again for about 40–60 minutes.

5. Preheat the oven to 180°C fan. Once doubled in size, lightly dust with flour using a sieve. Bake in the oven for 20 minutes, turning the tray 5 minutes from the end – they should be lightly golden on top.

6. Take from the oven and put the bread rolls on wire racks to cool completely.

This bread was a viral hit, and when you make it you'll see why. It's really easy and tastes so good. This bread can be made sweet or savoury. It's gorgeous as a breakfast bread, sweet with jam or savoury with cheese. I hope you try it and love it too.

Healthy porridge bread

MAKES 1 LOAF

- 1 large tub of natural yoghurt (500ml)
- 1 egg, beaten
- 300g oats
- 2 teaspoons bicarbonate of soda
- 2 teaspoons mixed seeds (optional)
- ½ teaspoon salt (optional)
- 1 tablespoon brown sugar (optional)

1. Preheat the oven to 180°C fan. Grease and line a 900g loaf tin.
2. Put the yoghurt and beaten egg into a bowl and stir well. Mix the oats, bicarbonate of soda, seeds and salt in a separate bowl, then add to the yoghurt mixture and stir thoroughly. Pour the mix into the prepared loaf tin.
3. Bake for 30 minutes at 180°C fan, then reduce the temperature to 150°C fan and bake for a further 30 minutes. Leave to cook in the tin for 15 minutes, then place on a wire rack to cool completely.

 STORAGE:
Store in an airtight container in a cupboard for 3 days.

 TO FREEZE:
Slice the porridge bread and freeze the slices flat in a labelled ziplock bag for up to 3 months.

 TO DEFROST:
Defrost in an airtight container overnight.

Prep time. **15 mins**   Cook time. **60 mins**

I've been eating this bread for as long as I can remember. My mum, Breda, would make it on a school day and it would disappear within an hour – with six kids in the house growing up, homemade bakes didn't last long. We'd have it warm with lashings of butter. I make this now for my kids and we still call it spotted dog – the raisins give it a spotty look like a dalmatian. It's a gorgeous bread to make and share with kids, and one they might even make with their own kids one day.

Nana Breda's spotted dog (sweet raisin bread)

MAKES 1 LOAF

450g self-raising flour
1 teaspoon bicarbonate of soda
1 teaspoon baking powder
50g sugar

110g salted butter, at room temperature
110g raisins
300ml whole milk
2 eggs, beaten

1. Preheat the oven to 200°C fan. Sieve the self-raising flour, bicarbonate of soda, baking powder and sugar into a mixing bowl. Add the butter and work it into the flour with your fingertips until it resembles coarse sand. Stir in the raisins.

2. Measure the milk into a jug and whisk in the eggs. Pour this into the mixing bowl and bring together with a fork. The dough should be soft but not too sticky. Add more liquid if it's dry or more flour if it's sticky.

3. Flour a flat baking tray and turn the dough onto the tray. Pat the dough into a round shape using your hands, then dip a knife into the flour bag and mark a cross on the top. Bake for 30–40 minutes. When it's baked, tap the bottom – it should sound hollow.

4. Leave to cool on a wire rack for at least 30 minutes. Enjoy with lashings of butter.

STORAGE:
The bread will keep in an airtight container for up to 3 days.

TO FREEZE:
Once completely cooled, cut the bread into slices and freeze in labelled ziplock bags for up to 3 months.

TO DEFROST:
Take the number of slices you need and either defrost in a container for an hour or two, or pop into the toaster from frozen.

 Prep time. **15 mins** Cook time. **30 mins**

I can't think of brown bread without thinking of my granny. She never made one loaf, but four at a time. She would keep one out and freeze the other three so she had a constant supply of her homemade bread.

I have so many fond memories of my granny baking. Her kitchen always smelled amazing and her cakes, breads and jams were just delicious. She was an amazing woman and in her kitchen nothing went to waste.

Granny's brown bread

MAKES 1 LOAF

FOR THE DRY INGREDIENTS
250g coarse wholemeal flour
60g plain flour
1 teaspoon baking powder
1 teaspoon bicarbonate of soda
1 tablespoon dark brown sugar (optional)
½ teaspoon salt

FOR THE WET INGREDIENTS
300ml buttermilk, plus a little extra if necessary
1½ tablespoons vegetable oil
1 egg

OPTIONAL TOPPING
½ tablespoon porridge oats

1. Preheat the oven to 190°C fan and grease and line a 900g loaf tin. Put both the flours, the baking powder, bicarbonate of soda, brown sugar (if using) and salt into a bowl, and mix to combine.

2. In a jug, whisk together the buttermilk, vegetable oil and egg. Make a well in the centre of the dry ingredients and add the buttermilk mix. Using a wooden spoon, mix gently and quickly until you have achieved a nice dropping consistency. Add a little bit more buttermilk if necessary.

3. Pour the mix into the loaf tin and sprinkle the porridge oats evenly on top, (if using). Bake for 60–70 minutes, turning halfway through.

4. To check that the loaf is properly cooked, tip it out of the tin and tap the base. It should sound hollow. If it doesn't, return it to the oven for another 5 minutes. When cooked, tip out on to a wire rack and leave to cool completely.

STORAGE:
Store in an airtight container for up to 3 days.

TO FREEZE:
Slice the bread and lay it flat in a labelled ziplock bag. Store in the freezer for up to 3 months.

TO DEFROST:
Defrost in an airtight container overnight.

TIP:
To make your own buttermilk, just add 1 tablespoon of white vinegar or lemon juice to 300ml of regular milk – it will sour instantly and mimic buttermilk.

Prep time. **15 mins**   Cook time. **70 mins**

This is usually eaten for breakfast or as a lazy brunch bread in Ireland. It is one of the best ways to use up leftover mashed potato. I often make mashed potatoes just for this recipe… it's so good. I'll double the amounts and freeze the extra for brunch another day.

Traditionally potato bread was made on a cast-iron griddle pan over the fire. Recipes for this don't always have egg added, but I like it – you can leave it out if you wish.

Irish potato bread

MAKES 4

250g potatoes (or leftover mash)
½ teaspoon salt

60g plain flour
1 egg, beaten

1. For raw potatoes, wash, peel and boil until tender, then drain and mash in a large bowl. Using the potatoes while still warm will give your bread a lighter texture.
2. Put the mashed potatoes into a mixing bowl along with the salt, flour and egg. Using a wooden spoon, mix until it forms a soft dough.
3. Tip the dough out on to a lightly floured surface and shape into a round, roughly 1cm thick. Use a sharp knife to cut a cross through the dough, dividing it into 4 equal wedges.
4. Heat a griddle or a flat, heavy-based frying pan on a medium-high heat.
5. Lightly oil and cook the slices for 4–5 minutes each side. They will be quite soft, so handle them carefully.
6. Allow to cool slightly on a rack. To serve, I like to warm a knob of butter in a frying pan and fry the bread on both sides.

STORAGE:
The bread will keep in an airtight container in the fridge for up to 3 days.

TO FREEZE:
Freeze the cooled loaves in labelled ziplock bags for up to 3 months.

TO DEFROST:
Defrost in the fridge overnight or cook from frozen. Fry or toast to your liking.

Prep time. **30 mins**   Cook time. **10 mins**

My good friend Laura gave me this recipe – she likes to add yeast and baking powder for an extra lift, and it really helps. These breads are so soft, fluffy and delicious that they will bring your curry to the next level!

I love making these with the kids. Traditionally, naans are a teardrop shape but we make all sorts of interesting shapes. Try hearts, triangles or even try shaping them into your favourite country! Great fun.

Naan breads

MAKES 6

125ml warm water (36°C)
1 × 7g sachet of dried yeast
2 teaspoons sugar
300g strong bread flour, plus extra for dusting
½ teaspoon salt
½ teaspoon baking powder
25g butter, melted
150g plain yoghurt

1. Measure the warm water into a jug and add the yeast and 1 teaspoon of sugar. Leave to activate for 15 minutes.

2. Measure the flour, salt, baking powder and the other teaspoon of sugar into a big bowl, and stir well to combine. When the yeast is ready, make a well in the flour and pour in the butter, yoghurt and yeasty liquid. Mix with a fork until the dough comes together. If it seems a little wet, add a spoonful of flour – if it seems a little dry, add a small spoonful of water. The dough should be soft but not too sticky.

3. Knead the dough in the bowl with your hands, then dust the worktop and tip the dough out. Knead by hand for a good 10 minutes, or in a standing mixer for 5–10 minutes. Oil a second mixing bowl and put the dough ball in it. Cover with a clean tea towel and leave for an hour to double in size.

4. Cut the dough into 6 equal pieces, place them on a floured baking tray and cover the tray with a damp tea towel to keep moist. Next, heat a large non-stick frying pan on a high heat. Take one piece of dough and roll it out into a teardrop shape, trying to keep the dough ½cm thick all over. Once the pan is hot, gently add the naan. Allow it to cook without oil for about 3 minutes, letting it puff up, then flip it over and cook for another 3–4 minutes until it's thoroughly cooked and has some charred spots.

5. Place the cooked naans on a clean tea towel and cover to keep warm while you cook the rest.

STORAGE:
Store the naans in an airtight container in a cupboard for up to 3 days.

TO FREEZE:
Freeze the cooled naan breads in a labelled ziplock bag for up to 3 months.

TO DEFROST:
Defrost in the fridge overnight, or reheat in the oven from frozen for about 10 minutes at 180°C fan.

Prep time. **15 mins**   Cook time. **25 mins plus prove time**

Easy cheesy rolls for the days when you run out of fresh bread!! Or if you want your kids to go to school with home-made bread, these are a fantastic option. We made these in my online kids' cooking class to go with a cheeseboard, and the kids were so impressed with themselves. It's a great starter bread for kids to make.

Easy cheese rolls

MAKES 8 ROLLS

300g self-raising flour (or use plain flour and 2 teaspoons of baking powder)
80g strong Cheddar cheese, grated, plus 2 tablespoons extra to top the rolls
½ teaspoon salt
330g thick Greek yoghurt

1. Preheat the oven to 200°C fan and line a baking tray with baking parchment.
2. Put the flour, 80g of cheese, salt and yoghurt into a mixing bowl. Use a wooden spoon or spatula to mix the dough together. Once it's looking lumpy, go in with your hands to bring it together into a rough dough.
3. Divide the dough into 8 equal pieces, then form them into rolls. Try not to handle the dough too much – that's the secret to a light roll! Arrange the rolls on your lined baking tray, leaving a little space between them so they have room to rise.
4. Top with the rest of the grated cheese and bake for 20 minutes, until they're looking lovely and golden. Remove from the oven and let them cool slightly on the tray, then devour!

STORAGE:
Store in an airtight container in the cupboard for up to 3 days.

TO FREEZE:
Once cooled, freeze the cheese rolls in a labelled ziplock bag for up to 3 months.

TO DEFROST:
Defrost in the fridge overnight.

Prep time. **15 mins**   Cook time. **20 mins**

Chapter 10

Sneaky Sweet Stuff

Beetroot is such a gorgeous root vegetable. It's naturally sweet and earthy, and it's great to bake with. When I was a child I used to eat whole pickled beetroots from the jar. My mum would serve them with a cold salad and I loved how they would turn all the food on plate pink. These days I like to buy Irish-grown raw beetroots and steam them. I sometimes even pickle my own.

My son Hamish loves this so much that I've named it after him. I make a double batch once a month, and I often put them in his lunchbox as a treat. I once forgot to add eggs but they still turned out great, more fudgy and yum. So eggs are optional.

Hamish's beetroot & chocolate traybake

MAKES 12

150g cooked and peeled beetroot, quartered
2 eggs (optional)
150ml milk
1 teaspoon vanilla extract
225g self-raising flour

100g sugar
25g cocoa powder
100g butter, melted
50g white chocolate chips (optional)

1. Preheat the oven to 170°C fan and line a 20cm square baking tray with baking parchment. Put the beetroot, eggs (if using), milk and vanilla into a blender and blend until smooth and pink.
2. Sieve the self-raising flour, sugar and cocoa powder into a mixing bowl, and mix well. Pour in the pink beetroot mix, and add the melted butter and the white chocolate chips. Gently mix until there are no dry bits of flour remaining.
3. Pour the mixture into the lined baking tray and bake for approximately 25–30 minutes. Check it is cooked by inserting a cocktail stick – when it comes out clean it's ready.
4. Allow to cool, then cut into 12 squares.

STORAGE:
Store the squares in an airtight container for up to 5 days.

TO FREEZE:
Freeze in labelled ziplock bags for up to 3 months.

TO DEFROST:
Defrost overnight in an airtight container on the worktop.

TIP:
I like to use vacuum-packed (pre-cooked) beetroots. But if you're using raw beetroot to begin with, steam, roast or boil them until completely cooked. Then peel and let them cool.

BONUS TIP:
This recipe can be baked as 12 muffins too!

Prep time. **20 mins**   Cook time. **30 mins**

Sweet potato is a super vegetable to bake with – try adding it to muffins and cakes too. I love to use it because it is a great source of fibre and great for the gut. I have been making these pancakes for my kids for many years. The flavour of the sweet potato is subtle in the pancakes, so it's not very noticeable. Worth trying if you have a picky eater.

Sweet potato & cinnamon pancakes

MAKES 12

2 tablespoons butter, melted
250g self-raising flour
1 teaspoon bicarbonate of soda
2 tablespoons sugar
½ teaspoon ground cinnamon

150g cooked sweet potato cubes (steamed or boiled)
250ml milk, and maybe a bit more
1 egg
1 tablespoon lemon juice or white vinegar

1. Sieve the flour, bicarbonate of soda, sugar and cinnamon into a mixing bowl.
2. Blend the sweet potato, milk, egg and lemon juice together until smooth, then combine with the flour mix. The mix should drop off a spoon like thick cream. Add more milk if it's too thick, or a bit more flour if it's too thin. Stir in the melted butter.
3. Warm a non-stick frying pan on a medium heat. Lightly oil the pan. Spoon on small mounds of the batter, and smooth them down to a round shape. Cook for 3–4 minutes, until bubbles form, then flip them over and cook for a further minute. Repeat with the rest of the mixture.

STORAGE:
The pancakes will keep in an airtight container in the fridge for up to 3 days.

TO FREEZE:
Freeze the pancakes flat in labelled ziplock bags for up to 3 months.

TO DEFROST:
Defrost in an airtight container on the worktop overnight. To reheat, pop them into the microwave or toaster for a few seconds.

TIP:
I like to steam a few sweet potatoes and have them in the fridge to use in recipes like this and my hand pies (see page 55).

Image on page 223

Prep time. 20 mins   Cook time. 20 mins

These make the perfect green breakfast pancake stack for St Patrick's day, the day where we are all that bit extra-Irish. Spinach is also a great ingredient to get goodness and greenness into your bakes. It works really well with bananas, and makes a fun breakfast all year round.

Spinach & banana pancakes

MAKES 12

40g baby spinach, washed
1 banana
1 egg
150g plain yoghurt
100ml milk

240g plain flour
1 teaspoon baking powder
1 teaspoon bicarbonate of soda
2 tablespoons sugar
oil, for cooking

1. Tip the spinach into a blender along with the banana, egg, yoghurt and milk, and blend until really smooth and bright green.
2. Sieve the flour, baking powder, bicarbonate of soda and sugar into a mixing bowl and mix really well with a spoon.
3. Pour in the green liquid mix and gently stir the batter until no flour remains visible.
4. Warm a frying pan on a medium heat and oil it lightly. Add 2 dessertspoons of batter per pancake to the frying pan and use the back of the spoon to make them round. Cook 3 or 4 pancakes at a time if they fit into the pan.
5. Cook until little bubbles appear, then flip the pancakes and cook for a further minute or two until cooked through. Serve warm, with berries, bananas or any of your favourite toppings.

STORAGE:
Store in an airtight container for up to 3 days.

TO FREEZE:
Freeze in a labelled ziplock bag for up to 3 months.

TO DEFROST:
Defrost in the fridge overnight, or pop them into the toaster from frozen.

Image on page 222

Prep time. **15 mins**   Cook time. **20 mins**

This is the perfect Sunday bake when you're at home and need something sweet but with some added goodness. Chickpeas are a great source of fibre, and while these are still a sweet treat, they are a nourishing ingredient to add to your bakes.

Chickpea & raspberry blondies

MAKES 9 SQUARES

- 1 × 400g tin of chickpeas, drained
- 1 teaspoon vanilla extract
- 1 teaspoon baking powder
- ½ teaspoon bicarbonate of soda
- ¼ teaspoon salt
- 75g sugar
- 2 eggs
- 50g cashew nuts or ground almonds
- 40g butter, at room temperature
- 50g plain flour
- 30g white chocolate chips
- 20 raspberries, fresh or frozen

1. Preheat the oven to 180°C fan. Line a 20cm square baking tin with baking parchment.
2. Blend the chickpeas, vanilla, baking powder, bicarbonate of soda, salt, sugar, eggs, cashew nuts and butter in a processor until really smooth.
3. Pour the mix into a mixing bowl, then sieve in the plain flour and gently mix to combine. Transfer the mix to the baking tin, sprinkle over the white chocolate chips and press the raspberries evenly on top.
4. Bake for 25 minutes. The blondies will look a little underdone when you take them out, but they firm up while cooling. Once cooled, divide into 9 even squares.

STORAGE:
These blondies will keep in an airtight container in the fridge for up to 3 days.

TO FREEZE:
Freeze flat in labelled ziplock bags for up to 3 months.

TO DEFROST:
Defrost in an airtight container on the worktop overnight.

Prep time. **15 mins**   Cook time. **25 mins plus cooling time**

I have grown courgettes in my garden and it's not that difficult to do! They were small courgettes, but I was still very proud of them. Courgette has a fairly neutral flavour, so it's a good vegetable to bake with and you can add whatever flavours you like to it, but we particularly like these lemony muffins.

Courgette & lemon muffins

**MAKES 12
REGULAR MUFFINS**

250g courgettes
250g self-raising flour
150g caster sugar
1 teaspoon baking powder

a pinch of salt
zest of 1 lemon
100g milk
100g vegetable oil
1 egg

1. Preheat the oven to 180°C fan and line a 12-hole muffin tin with paper cases.
2. Wash and dry the courgettes and coarsely grate them. Place the grated courgette in a sieve and press it to get rid of some of the excess liquid as best you can.
3. Sieve the flour, sugar, baking powder and salt into a large mixing bowl and give it a mix. Zest in the lemon and mix in the grated courgette.
4. In a jug, whisk together the milk, oil and egg. Pour it into the mixing bowl and stir until all the flour is mixed in. The mix will be lumpy, that's fine.
5. Spoon the mix into the paper cases and bake in the oven for 25 minutes, until nicely golden on top.

STORAGE:
These muffins will keep well for up to 3 days in an airtight container.

TO FREEZE:
Freeze flat in labelled ziplock bags for up to 3 months.

TO DEFROST:
Defrost in an airtight container on the worktop overnight.

TIP:
For an optional drizzle to finish, mix 100g of caster sugar with the juice of 2 lemons in a saucepan over a low heat until the sugar has dissolved. Drizzle this over the muffins as they're cooling.

Image on page 228

 Prep time. **15 mins**   Cook time. **25 mins**

It's safe to say that cookies are always welcome in our house. These are soft and fudgy and delicious as a snack. Last summer we headed out on a beach adventure for the day. We packed a big picnic with sandwiches, fruit, a flask for tea and these cookies. Eating them on a picnic blanket with your family is highly recommended.

Black bean & chocolate chip cookies

MAKES 12

250g oats
1 × 400g tin of black beans, drained well
125ml maple syrup or honey
2 heaped tablespoons cocoa powder

40g butter, at room temperature
80g chocolate chips

TO DECORATE:
70g chocolate, melted

1. Preheat the oven to 180°C fan, and line two baking trays with baking parchment.
2. Put half the oats into a blender. Add the drained black beans, maple syrup, cocoa powder and butter and process until fairly smooth.
3. Scoop the mix into a mixing bowl, and stir through the other half of the oats and the chocolate chips.
4. Divide the mix into 12 balls. Place on the baking trays and push down to flatten. If you have a cookie cutter, use it to mould them into nice round shapes if not, do your best to shape them with your hands. Bake for 15 minutes. Let them cool on the trays for a few minutes, then transfer to a wire rack.
5. Melt the chocolate in the microwave in short bursts or in a small pot on a very low heat. Drizzle the cooled cookies with melted chocolate. Serve with cold milk or a hot coffee.

STORAGE:
These cookies will keep in an airtight container for up to 5 days.

TO FREEZE:
Freeze in labelled ziplock bags for up to 3 months.

TO DEFROST:
Defrost in an airtight container overnight.

Image on page 229

Prep time. 15 mins   Cook time. 15 mins plus decorating time

Carrot cake is a classic bake, although this recipe is my own healthier version. My granny and my mum always made it, and now it's lovely to carry on the tradition and teach my kids too. This is a lovely bake to make with your kids on a rainy afternoon when you've nowhere else to be. When it's ready to slice, turn off the screens, pour cups of tea or milk and enjoy it together with laughs and giggles.

Carrot cake with maple & orange cream cheese frosting

MAKES 12 SQUARES

50g raisins
200g plain flour
100g wholemeal flour
2 teaspoons baking powder
1 tablespoon ground cinnamon
¼ teaspoon mixed spice
150g carrots, grated
125g plain yoghurt

100ml olive oil
3 eggs
140ml maple syrup or honey

FOR THE FROSTING
250g cream cheese
2 tablespoons maple syrup or honey
zest of ½ an orange

1. Preheat the oven to 170°C fan, and line a 20cm baking tin with baking parchment.

2. Soak the raisins in a small bowl of boiling water for 30 minutes – this rehydrates the raisins, making them nice and plump. Then strain the raisins and set aside.

3. Measure the plain flour, wholemeal flour, baking powder, cinnamon and mixed spice into a large mixing bowl and mix really well. Then stir through the grated carrot and the plump raisins.

4. In a jug, whisk together the yoghurt, oil and eggs and maple syrup or honey. Pour this into the mixing bowl and stir until there is no dry flour remaining. Transfer into the baking tin and bake for 30 minutes. To check it's cooked, use a cocktail stick – when it comes out clean the cake is ready.

5. Let the cake cool in the tin for 5 minutes, then transfer to a wire rack to cool completely.

6. To make the frosting, whisk together the cream cheese, maple syrup and orange zest. Pour over the cake and use a spatula or spoon to smooth it out. Cut into 12 squares.

STORAGE:
The squares will keep in an airtight container for up to 3 days.

TO FREEZE:
First freeze the frosted squares on a tray uncovered, then once frozen, transfer them into labelled ziplock bags and put them back into the freezer. They are good for up to 3 months.

TO DEFROST:
Defrost overnight in an airtight container on the worktop.

TIP:
This cake can be made in a round or a square tin. I like the square shape because it's easy to line the square tin and portion for the freezer.

Chocolate mousse is such a luxurious treat, and you won't believe how amazing these pots taste until you try them! They are smooth, creamy and delicious, and best of all they are made with a secret veggie ingredient … butternut squash. You must try them. I shared this recipe on my Instagram page and it was a viral hit!

Super-secret chocolate mousse pots

MAKES 6 POTS

300g butternut squash, peeled and diced
150g chocolate (I use milk chocolate)
50g butter (I use salted butter)
100ml cream, whipped (or vanilla yoghurt if you prefer)

1. Cook the butternut squash – steam it if you can, or boil it until soft and strain. Put it into a food processor while it's still warm.
2. Melt the chocolate and butter in the microwave or in a bowl over a pan of simmering water. Blend with the butternut squash until silky-smooth, then pour into a bowl and leave on the worktop to cool completely, covered loosely with a clean tea towel.
3. Whip the cream to soft peaks, then fold through the mousse. Spoon into six pots and pop them into the fridge to set for at least 3 hours, or overnight if you can.
4. Serve topped with fresh raspberries and an extra dollop of cream if you fancy.

 STORAGE:
The mousse pots will keep in the fridge for up to 3 days.

 TO FREEZE:
Wrap the individual pots in cling film or similar. They will freeze perfectly for up to 3 months.

 TO DEFROST:
Defrost them in the fridge overnight.

Prep time. **25 mins**   Chill time. **3 hours**

Protein snacks are all the rage at the moment. You can pick up energy bars and balls in the shops, but you will pay well for them. You can easily make your own high protein snacks, and adding lentils is a budget-friendly way to up the protein punch.

Lentil & lemon energy balls

MAKES 15

- 100g red lentils, uncooked
- 100g rolled oats
- 90g peanut butter, or any nut butter
- 3 tablespoons honey or maple syrup
- 1 tablespoon ground flaxseed
- zest of 1 lemon
- ½ teaspoon ground cinnamon
- ¼ teaspoon ground ginger
- 50g dark chocolate, melted, to drizzle (optional)

1. To cook the lentils, place them in a saucepan with 200ml of water. Bring to the boil, then reduce the heat, cover, and simmer for about 15 minutes, until the lentils are very tender and the water has been absorbed. Set aside to cool.
2. Put the oats into a food processor and blend to a coarse powder. Add the cooked lentils and the rest of the ingredients, except the chocolate, and blend until the mixture clumps together – if it seems very dry, add a teaspoon of boiled water, blend again and test.
3. Keeping your hands damp, roll the mixture into balls about the size of golf balls.
4. Melt the chocolate, either in the microwave or in a bowl over a pan of boiling water. Drizzle the chocolate over the balls and place them in the fridge to set.

STORAGE:
Store in an airtight container in the fridge for up to 5 days.

TO FREEZE:
Freeze in labelled ziplock bags for up to 3 months.

TO DEFROST:
The energy balls defrost within 2 hours on the worktop.

Prep time. **20 mins**   Chill time. **20 mins**

Pumpkins are definitely seasonal and are all the go in the lead up to Hallowe'en. Pumpkin purée isn't easy to come by in Ireland, so I make my own to add to bakes in the autumn. These pumpkin cheesecakes are really easy to make, and best of all they require absolutely no baking!!

Mini pumpkin cheesecakes (no-bake)

MAKES 12

FOR THE BISCUIT BASE
200g digestives
100g unsalted butter, melted

FOR THE PUMPKIN PURÉE
½ a small pumpkin, to make 150g purée
1 teaspoon ground cinnamon
¼ teaspoon mixed spice
25g icing sugar

FOR THE CHEESECAKE FILLING
300g full-fat soft cream cheese
50g icing sugar
1 teaspoon vanilla extract
150ml double cream

1. To roast the pumpkin, remove the seeds, keep the skin on and place flesh side down on a roasting tray. Roast for 30 minutes at 180°C fan until the flesh is completely soft. Scoop out and blend with the cinnamon, mixed spice and icing sugar. Alternatively, remove the skin and seeds, dice and steam for 30 minutes until completely soft, then blend with the cinnamon, mixed spice and icing sugar. Set aside to cool completely.

2. To make the biscuit base, line a 12-hole cupcake tray with cupcake cases. Blitz the biscuits in a food processor and mix with the melted butter. Divide the biscuit mix between the 12 holes, pushing down with the back of a spoon or the end of a rolling pin. Put the tray in the fridge to set while you make the filling.

3. In a large bowl, whisk together the cream cheese, icing sugar and vanilla until smooth. Whip the double cream separately to stiff peaks in another bowl and fold through the mixture. Fold through the pumpkin purée to leave flecks of orange in the mix, then spoon the mixture into the 12 cupcake cases and smooth over.

4. Set the cheesecakes in the fridge for at least 3–4 hours or in the freezer for 2–3 hours.

5. To serve the cheesecakes, take them out of the paper cases.

STORAGE:
The cheesecakes will keep in an airtight container in the fridge for up to 3 days.

TO FREEZE:
Freeze in an airtight container for up to 3 months.

TO DEFROST:
Defrost in the fridge for 2 hours, then serve.

TIP:
I like to use small pumpkins for sweet baking. If you can't find pumpkin, use butternut squash or sweet potatoes. Any leftover pumpkin can be used for a delicious soup, or roasted for salads or a side dish for dinner.

Prep time. **35 mins**   Chill time. **4 hours**

Meal Plans

5-Day Lunchbox Plan

I've been making my homemade lunchbox snacks for a few years now. It takes time to get into the habit of making them and keeping it up throughout the year, and I find a visual plan helps me keep on track. This plan offers variety use it as a guide and make your own plan of the things your kids will eat.

Note It's important to offer fresh fruit and/or vegetables along with the lunchbox snacks. I like to add yoghurt occasionally, and water every day to drink.

The recipes for each of these snacks are in this cookbook. Mix and match and take some ideas from my Sneaky Sweet Stuff section too.

Day 1

- ☐ Mini sausage rolls
- ☐ Oatcakes with butterbean hummus
- ☐ Apple & raisin slice

NOTES

→ The sausage rolls offer a protein-packed bite, while the oatcakes and butterbean hummus provide a filling and fibre-rich option.

→ The apple and raisin slice adds a sweet treat at lunchtime.

Day 2

- ☐ Mini ham & cheese quiches
- ☐ Sweet potato & carrot fritters
- ☐ Seed & date flapjacks

NOTES

→ The mini quiches are full of protein, perfect for keeping stomachs full throughout the day.

→ The fritters are a great veggie-packed side, and the flapjacks are a sweet, high-energy snack to round off the lunch.

Day 3

- ☐ Pizza scones
- ☐ Courgette and sweetcorn muffins
- ☐ Nut-free energy balls

NOTES

→ The pizza scones offer a savoury twist, with cheese and sun-dried-tomato pesto.

→ The muffins are a healthy, veg-filled option that can be enjoyed hot or cold.

→ Energy balls are a great grab-and-go snack, rich in fibre and seeds, and perfect to keep energy up in the afternoon.

Day 4

- ☐ Pesto & cheese pastry scrolls
- ☐ Sweet potato & goat's cheese hand pies
- ☐ Mini sweet scones with raspberry chia seed jam

NOTES

→ The pesto and cheese pastry scrolls are flaky and savoury.

→ The sweet potato and goat's cheese hand pies are rich and hearty, with a lovely cheesy, veggie filling.

→ The mini sweet scones are great with butter and homemade raspberry chia seed jam.

Day 5

- ☐ Pea, mint & feta pancakes
- ☐ Courgette & sweetcorn muffins
- ☐ School cookies

NOTES

→ The pea, mint and feta pancakes offer a savoury option with fresh flavours.

→ The courgette and sweetcorn muffins are delicious, light and vegetable-packed.

→ These school cookies bring a special end to the week.

Family Dinner Meal Plan

I absolutely love a meal plan or guide to follow during busy weeks. The beauty of the recipes in this book is that if you get into the habit of making extra for the freezer you'll have meals made and frozen, ready to grab when you need them.

Be sure to add a variety of vegetables on the side to make the meals nutritionally balanced. I like to add some of the following: steamed broccoli, cauliflower, peas, sweetcorn and carrots.

There are 30 dinner recipes in this book, so come up with a plan that works for your family. You can decide whether to plan for slow cooker, air fryer, traybakes or pies. Here are 4 meal plans to get you started. The recipes for each of these dinners are in this cookbook.

Meal Plans

Plan One

Monday	**Slow cooker** 'Cowboy supper' – sausage & bean casserole
Tuesday	**Air fryer** Chicken goujons with mushy peas & mashed potato
Wednesday	**Air fryer** Pork & apple burgers with sweet potato chips
Thursday	**Slow cooker** Beef & chorizo chilli with rice
Friday	**Air fryer** Homemade chips, eggs & beans
Saturday	**Slow cooker** BBQ pulled pork on soft bread rolls
Sunday	**Pie/Traybake** Beef stroganoff cottage pie

Plan Two

Monday	**Slow cooker** Red lentil dahl
Tuesday	**Air fryer** Easy beanie patties
Wednesday	**Air fryer** Mexican beef fajitas
Thursday	**Slow cooker** Chickpea & butternut squash curry with rice
Friday	**Pie/Traybake** Fish pie
Saturday	**Slow cooker** Butter chicken curry with rice
Sunday	**Pie/Traybake** Chicken & leek pie

Plan Three

Monday	**Slow cooker** Veggie bolognaise
Tuesday	**Air fryer** Quick turkey meatballs on a sub roll with tomato sauce
Wednesday	**Pie/Traybake** Creamy butternut squash & mushroom filo pie
Thursday	**Slow cooker** Moroccan lamb tagine with couscous

Meal Plans

Friday	**Air fryer**	Crispy sweet chilli chicken with noodles
Saturday	**Slow cooker**	Saucy meatballs with pasta
Sunday	**Pie/Traybake**	Italian sausage, tomato and polenta pie
Monday	**Slow cooker**	Butter chicken curry
Tuesday	**Air fryer**	Falafel, herb yoghurt with pitta breads (v)
Wednesday	**Pie/Traybake**	Bobotie
Thursday	**Slow cooker**	Beef & chorizo chilli with rice
Friday	**Air fryer**	Soy and honey salmon & greens
Saturday	**Slow cooker**	BBQ pulled pork on soft bread rolls
Sunday	**Pie/Traybake**	Sweet potato, feta & spinach lasagne

Plan Four

 **TIPS**

→ FROM THE FREEZER: *If you have made any of the dinners or elements of the dinners suggested, defrost or prepare as instructed in the recipe in this book. Planning meals means you'll get the most from the recipes you've already made and frozen.*

→ REMEMBER TO DEFROST: *Keep your meal plan somewhere where it's easy to find and check. Put it on your phone or on a blackboard or stick it on the fridge – that way it will help you remember to defrost the specific meal overnight in the fridge.*

→ SHOPPING LIST: *The weekly meal plan will dictate your shopping list. Plan ahead and include breakfast, lunch and any sweet or bread baking you wish to do. It will save you time and money in the long run.*

Thanks a million x

My partner in crime

To my husband and my best friend Mike. Who's never doubted or questioned my career choices. Who's supported me from day one and encouraged me to follow my dreams. I needed to put my head down this year and you stepped up to the plate. Thanks for doing all the laundry, helping the kids with homework and manning all the school runs and activities. And most of all thanks for washing the pile of dishes for well over 100 test recipes for my book and never complaining! You're my hero. xx

My kids

Meabh you made me a mum just over a decade ago and you have made me so proud every day since. Thank you for being so sweet, positive and supportive every day. You're my number one food critic, if you liked the recipe it made the cut! X

Hamish thank you for testing me in the kitchen. Your unwillingness to try new foods has pushed me to be very clever and creative. You are the inspiration for many of my sneaky veg recipes!! So thank you for that. You're such a kind, curious and independent boy, and the best pizza chef. X

Mum

To my kind, caring, creative and beautiful mother Breda. Who tells me repeatedly how proud she is of me. Thank you for being my number one cheerleader and for testing my bread recipes. Thanks to my sister Eithne, brothers Darren, Shay and Aidan and my in-laws, I'm very lucky to have an incredibly supportive loving family.

My followers, my online family

I started my page in 2021 with no idea what I was doing or where it would go. I shared recipes that I made for my family, quick, easy and freezer-friendly. My messaging became clearer and I started to reach a bigger audience and you came and followed in your droves. And I was bowled over and still am.

Thank you for joining me and following along. Thank you for making my recipes and telling me about it. Your daily photos and messages mean everything to me. Hearing that your kids enjoy my recipes and you make them on repeat, keeps me going every day.

My fellow creators

I'm very fortunate to have found a very supportive bunch of like-minded people on social media. Thank you Ciara, Nicole, Jen, Maria, Orla, Rachel, Nathan and all the gang for being so supportive. Content creation can be a solitary space but it's great having that community to reach out to.

Literary Agent

When people genuinely believe in you, it is something very special! My agent Sarah Hornsley didn't hesitate to take me on and help me realize my dreams. Thank you Sarah for the brilliant concept for this book and your swift and efficient work. It is very reassuring having you on my side to keep me right. I can't thank you enough. Thank you so much Ciara Attwell for being so kind and introducing me to Sarah.

Publisher and editor

Ione Walder, I thank my lucky stars that you picked up my cookbook proposal in 2024. For this book to work it was imperative that my editor really understood the concept and the need for this book in every family home. Ione from the very first call it was clear that you got it. Thank you for seeing the potential in me and for trusting me. You have been so lovely and professional and supportive and made the whole experience very enjoyable.

Thank you Michael Joseph of Penguin Random House, it's been my honour to publish with such a prestigious international publisher, I'll be forever grateful.

Assistant editor

Thanks to Sukhmani Bhakar, for being super organized and keeping me informed of all the details especially on our London and Galway shoots. It was lovely to spend time with you in London and see the passion you have for your work.

Cookbook designer

Thank you to cookbook designer Sarah Fraser. Every book needs a vision and you got this one spot on, it has far exceeded my expectations! Thank you for travelling to Galway to immerse yourself in the beauty of Ireland for my shoot, for your expertise and well thought-out design, I love every detail.

Photographer

Ella Miller you are so unassuming for a woman with an incredible portfolio under your belt. I loved watching you work so effortlessly in London and Galway. You are a true talent, the photos are stunning and I think I'll get a few framed for the wall! Thank you to assistant photographer Rosie for all your hard work.

Food Stylist

I didn't realize that I wouldn't have to cook the recipes for the actual book and was thrilled to hear it would be taken care of professionally! Thank you so much Holly Cowgill for cooking and styling all of my recipes, you're so calm and considered it was a pleasure to watch you work. The food looks stunning! A pinch-me moment was sitting at the London studio with the shoot team eating my recipes for lunch cooked perfectly by you! Special thanks to your assistant Alice for her hard work also.

Prop stylist

Luis Peral, I wish you could come and style my life! You carefully choose every plate, cup, fork, background and detail in each of the photos. It's beautifully fresh, yet warm with the perfect palate to match. Thank you so much for your attention to detail and beautiful work.

Galway Location

Sarah O'Connell of the Burren House Project for allowing us to use your home, on the west coast, for the Galway shoot. We have known each other for a while and it was extra special to have the photos captured in your stunning home.

Personal stylist

Thank you Joanna Cluskey for taking me on a shopping spree around Galway. And for your expertise in choosing a gorgeous rail of considered clothes to wear, as well as clothes for my kids too. We've known each other for a good few years and it was really special to have you there to style me for the Galway shoot. Thank you to Harper Galway, An Standun, Spiddal and Rea Feather, Dublin, for kindly lending your beautiful pieces.

Makeup artist

Pauline Fletcher, so great to have your professional touch for my makeup on the Galway shoot. It made me feel confident and ready for the day and you were lovely to work with. Thank you so much.

Penguin campaign team, Ireland and London

Thank you to Cliona Lewis and Mubarak Elmubarak and the whole team for putting together an incredible exciting campaign to launch my cookbook! The most amazing opportunities, beyond my wildest dreams!! Thank you all so so much.

Index

A

ABC muffins **73**
air fryers **124–42**
American style 'weekend' pancakes with maple and bacon **22–3**
apples
    ABC muffins **73**
    apple and raisin slice **76**
    blueberry delight smoothie **95**
    mango tango smoothie **94**
    parsnip and apple soup **88**
    pork and apple burgers with sweet potato chips **127**
    totally tropical smoothie **94**
apricot and coconut bliss balls **78**
avocados
    chocolate and banana baked oats **27**
    huevos rancheros **33**

B

bacon
    American style 'weekend' pancakes with maple and bacon **22–3**
    chicken and leek pie **150–1**
    mini bacon and cheese quiches **42**
bananas
    ABC muffins **73**
    green hulk smoothie **99**
    'school morning' blender pancakes **24**
    spinach and banana pancakes **221**
    strawberry dream smoothie **95**
    totally tropical smoothie **94**
BBQ pulled pork on soft bread rolls **113**
beef
    beef and chorizo chilli con carne **105**
    beef stroganoff cottage pie **146–7**
    bobotie **156**
    meatloaf with tomato sauce and baby potatoes **142**
    Mexican beef fajitas **130**
    saucy meatballs with pasta **114**
beetroot
    and chocolate traybake **218**
    curry lentil pie **166**
berries
    blueberry breakfast bars **28**
    blueberry delight smoothie **95**
    frozen yoghurt bark **181**
    mixed berry compote **34**
    raspberry chia seed jam **20**
biscuits *see* cookies and biscuits
black beans
    black bean and chocolate chip cookies **227**
    easy beanie patties **133**
    red pepper and black bean enchiladas **162**
blondies: chickpea and raspberry **225**
blueberries
    blueberry delight smoothie **95**
    breakfast bars **28**
    lemon and blueberry mini loaves **79**
bobotie **156**
bolognaise: veggie **110**
bread
    easy cheese rolls **215**
    Granny's brown bread **208**
    gypsy bread with mixed berry compote **34**
    healthy porridge bread **205**
    Irish potato bread **211**
    miracle loaf (no-knead) **194**
    naan breads **213**
    Nana Breda's spotted dog **207**
    overnight 'fridge' focaccia **201**

Index

 pizza dough **196**
 super-soft bread rolls **203–4**
breakfasts **20–37**
broccoli
 salmon and broccoli frittata slices **59**
 soy and honey salmon with rice and greens **141**
brownies: double chocolate **190**
burgers
 easy beanie patties **133**
 pork and apple burgers with sweet potato chips **127**
butter chicken curry **116–17**
butterbeans
 Italian sausage polenta pie **154**
 oatcakes with butterbean hummus **46**
butternut squash
 chickpea and butternut squash curry **108**
 creamy butternut squash and mushroom filo pie **153**
 super-secret chocolate mousse pots **232**

C

cakes and bars
 ABC muffins **73**
 apple and raisin slice **76**
 blueberry breakfast bars **28**
 carrot cake with maple and orange cream cheese frosting **230**
 courgette and lemon muffins **226**
 courgette and sweetcorn muffins **57**
 crunch bars **170**
 double chocolate brownies **190**
 easy donuts **182**
 easy oat bars **67**
 Hamish's beetroot and chocolate traybake **218**
 lemon and blueberry mini loaves **79**
 mini pumpkin cheesecakes (no-bake) **237**
 mini vanilla cupcakes **186**
 no-bake bubble rice treat **175**
 no-bake caramel bars **175**
 raspberry and ricotta muffins with crumble topping **70**
 rocky road **185**
 seed and date flapjacks **66**
cannellini beans
 'cowboy supper' sausage and bean casserole **102**
 Italian sausage polenta pie **154**
caramel bars **175**
carrots
 ABC muffins **73**
 carrot cake with maple and orange cream cheese frosting **230**
 chicken noodle soup **90**
 'cowboy supper' sausage and bean casserole **102**
 minestrone soup **89**
 Moroccan lamb tagine with couscous **121**
 pesto and cheese pastry scrolls **48**
 red lentil dahl **106**
 sweet potato and carrot fritters **56**
 veggie bolognaise **110**
casserole: 'cowboy supper' sausage and bean **102**
cauliflower: curry lentil pie **166**
cheese
 cheesy potato waffles **36**
 courgette and sweetcorn muffins **57**
 easy cheese rolls **215**
 Italian sausage polenta pie **154**
 mini bacon and cheese quiches **42**
 pea, mint and feta pancakes **49**
 pesto and cheese pastry scrolls **48**
 pizza macaroni cheese **165**
 pizza scones **52**
 red pepper and black bean enchiladas **162**
 salmon and broccoli frittata slices **59**

sausage and egg muffin cupcakes **37**
sweet potato and goat's cheese hand pies **55**
sweet potato, feta and spinach lasagne **158–61**
sweetcorn and cheese fritters **31**

cheesecakes: mini pumpkin **237**

chicken
butter chicken curry **116–17**
chicken and leek pie **150–1**
chicken goujons with mushy peas and mashed potato **124–5**
chicken noodle soup **90**
creamy garlic and lemon chicken with buttery mash and veg **118**
crispy sweet chilli chicken with soy noodles **136–7**

chickpeas
chickpea and butternut squash curry **108**
chickpea and raspberry blondies **225**
falafel, herb yoghurt and pitta breads **139**

chilli con carne **105**

chips
homemade chips, eggs and beans **129**
sweet potato **127**

chocolate
black bean and chocolate chip cookies **227**
chocolate and banana baked oats **27**
crunch bars **170**
double chocolate brownies **190**
easy donuts **182**
Hamish's beetroot and chocolate traybake **218**
lentil and lemon energy balls **235**
Meabh's memory cookies **176**
no-bake bubble rice treat **189**
no-bake caramel bars **175**
rocky road **185**
super-secret chocolate mousse pots **232**

chorizo: beef and chorizo chilli con carne **105**

compote: mixed berry **34**

cookies and biscuits
black bean and chocolate chip cookies **227**
gingernut biscuits **172**
Meabh's memory cookies **176**
oatcakes with butterbean hummus **46**
school cookies **72**

cottage pie **146–7**

courgettes
courgette and lemon muffins **226**
courgette and sweetcorn muffins **57**
Italian sausage polenta pie **154**
minestrone soup **89**

couscous: Moroccan lamb tagine **121**

'cowboy supper' sausage and bean casserole **102**

creamy butternut squash and mushroom filo pie **153**

creamy garlic and lemon chicken with buttery mash and veg **118**

crêpes with raspberry chia seed jam **20**

crispy sweet chilli chicken with soy noodles **136–7**

crunch bars **170**

cupcakes: mini vanilla **186**

curried sweet potato and coconut soup **86**

curries
butter chicken with rice **116–17**
chickpea and butternut squash curry **108**
curry lentil pie **166**
red lentil dahl **106**

D

dahl: red lentil **106**

dates
no-bake caramel bars **175**
nut-free energy balls **62**
seed and date flapjacks **66**

defrosting **15**

donuts **182**

E

easy beanie patties 133
easy donuts 182
easy oat bars 67
eggs
    cheesy potato waffles 36
    homemade chips, eggs and beans 129
    huevos rancheros 33
    salmon and broccoli frittata slices 59
    sausage and egg muffin cupcakes 37
enchiladas: red pepper and black bean 162
energy balls
    lentil and lemon 235
    nut-free 62

F

fajitas: Mexican beef 130
falafel, herb yoghurt and pitta breads 139
feta
    pea, mint and feta pancakes 49
    red pepper and black bean enchiladas 162
    sweet potato, feta and spinach lasagne 158–61
filo pastry: creamy butternut squash and mushroom pie 153
fish
    fish pie 148
    salmon and broccoli frittata slices 59
flapjacks: seed and date 66
focaccia 201
freezing 15–17
frittata: salmon and broccoli 59
fritters: sweet potato and carrot 56
frozen yoghurt bark 181

G

gingernut biscuits 172
goat's cheese: sweet potato hand pies 55
Granny's brown bread 208
green hulk smoothie 99
gypsy bread with mixed berry compote 34

H

huevos rancheros 33
hummus: butterbean 46

I

Irish potato bread 211
Italian sausage polenta pie 154

J

jam: raspberry chia seed 20

K

kidney beans
    beef and chorizo chilli con carne 105
    huevos rancheros 33

L

lamb
    bobotie 156
    Moroccan lamb tagine with couscous 121
lasagne: sweet potato, feta and spinach 158–61
leeks: chicken and leek pie 150–1
lemon and blueberry mini loaves 79
lentils
    creamy butternut squash and mushroom filo pie 153
    curry lentil pie 166
    lentil and lemon energy balls 235
    red lentil dahl 106
    veggie bolognaise 110
lunchboxes 62–79, 240–1
lunchboxes: savoury 42–59

M

macaroni cheese 165
mango tango smoothie 94
Meabh's memory cookies 176
meal plans 240–5
meatballs
    with pasta 114
    quick turkey meatballs on a sub roll with tomato sauce 134
meatloaf with tomato sauce and baby potatoes 142
Mexican beef fajitas 130
mini bacon and cheese quiches 42
mini pumpkin cheesecakes (no-bake) 237
mini sausage rolls 42
mini sweet scones 63
muffins
    ABC muffins 73
    courgette and lemon 226
    courgette and sweetcorn 57
    raspberry and ricotta with crumble topping 70
    sausage and egg muffin cupcakes 37
mushrooms
    creamy butternut squash and mushroom filo pie 153
    veggie bolognaise 110

N

naan bread 213
Nana Breda's spotted dog 207
no-bake
    bubble rice treat 189
    caramel bars 175
    mini pumpkin cheesecakes 237
noodles
    chicken noodle soup 90
    crispy sweet chilli chicken with soy noodles 136–7
nut-free energy balls 62

O

oats
    apricot and coconut bliss balls 78
    black bean and chocolate chip cookies 227
    blueberry breakfast bars 28
    chocolate and banana baked oats 27
    easy oat bars 67
    healthy porridge bread 205
    lentil and lemon energy balls 235
    Meabh's memory cookies 176
    nut-free energy balls 62
    oatcakes with butterbean hummus 46
    school cookies 72
    'school morning' blender pancakes 24
    seed and date flapjacks 66

P

pancakes
    American style 'weekend' pancakes with maple and bacon 22–3
    crêpes with raspberry chia seed jam 20
    pea, mint and feta 49
    'school morning' blender pancakes 24
    spinach and banana 221
    sweet potato and cinnamon 220
parsnip and apple soup 88
pasta
    chicken noodle soup 90
    minestrone soup 89
    pizza macaroni cheese 165
    saucy meatballs 114
    veggie bolognaise 110
pastry
    chicken and leek pie 150–1
    creamy butternut squash and mushroom filo pie 153
    mini bacon and cheese quiches 42
    mini sausage rolls 42
    pesto and cheese pastry scrolls 48
    sweet potato and goat's cheese hand pies 55

peanut butter: crunch bars **170**

peas
- chicken goujons with mushy peas and mashed potato **124–5**
- pea, mint and feta pancakes **49**

peppers
- Italian sausage polenta pie **154**
- Mexican beef fajitas **130**
- red pepper and black bean enchiladas **162**
- roast tomato and red pepper soup **84**

pesto and cheese pastry scrolls **48**

pies
- beef stroganoff cottage pie **146–7**
- bobotie **156**
- chicken and leek **150–1**
- creamy butternut squash and mushroom filo pie **153**
- curry lentil pie **166**
- fish pie **148**
- Italian sausage polenta pie **154**
- sweet potato and goat's cheese hand pies **55**

pineapple smoothie **94**

pizza
- homemade **196–7**
- pizza macaroni cheese **165**
- pizza scones **52**

polenta: Italian sausage pie **154**

pork
- BBQ pulled pork on soft bread rolls **113**
- pork and apple burgers with sweet potato chips **127**

potatoes
- beef stroganoff cottage pie **146–7**
- cheesy potato waffles **36**
- chicken goujons with mushy peas and mashed potato **124–5**
- creamy garlic and lemon chicken with buttery mash and veg **118**
- curry lentil pie **166**
- fish pie **148**
- Irish potato bread **211**
- meatloaf with tomato sauce and baby potatoes **142**

pumpkin cheesecakes (no-bake) **237**

Q

quiches: mini bacon and cheese **45**

quick turkey meatballs **134**

R

raisin bread **207**

raspberries
- chickpea and raspberry blondies **225**
- raspberry and ricotta muffins **70**
- raspberry chia seed jam **20**

red lentil dahl **106**

relish: easy tomato **31**

rice
- beef and chorizo chilli con carne **105**
- butter chicken curry **116–17**
- chickpea and butternut squash curry **108**
- soy and honey salmon with rice and greens **141**

roast tomato and red pepper soup **84**

rocky road **185**

rolls
- easy cheese rolls **215**
- super-soft **203–4**

S

salmon
- and broccoli frittata slices **59**
- soy and honey salmon with rice and greens **141**

saucy meatballs with pasta **114**

sausages
- 'cowboy supper' sausage and bean casserole **102**

Italian sausage polenta pie 154
mini sausage rolls 42
sausage and egg muffin cupcakes 37
school cookies 72
'school morning' blender pancakes 24
scones
    mini sweet scones 63
    pizza scones 52
seeds
    apricot and coconut bliss balls 78
    blueberry delight smoothie 95
    green hulk smoothie 99
    nut-free energy balls 62
    raspberry chia seed jam 20
    school cookies 72
    seed and date flapjacks 66
slow cooker dinners 102–21
smoothies/smoothie pops 92
    blueberry delight 95
    green hulk 99
    mango tango 94
    strawberry dream 95
    totally tropical 94
soups
    chicken noodle 90
    curried sweet potato and coconut 86
    minestrone 89
    parsnip and apple 88
    roast tomato and red pepper 84
soy and honey salmon with rice and greens 141
spinach
    and banana pancakes 221
    green hulk smoothie 99
    sweet potato, feta and spinach lasagne 158–61
squash
    chickpea and butternut squash curry 108
    creamy butternut squash and mushroom filo pie 153
    mini pumpkin cheesecakes (no-bake) 237
    super-secret chocolate mousse pots 232
strawberry dream smoothie 95
sweet potato
    and carrot fritters 56
    chips 127
    and cinnamon pancakes 220
    'cowboy supper' sausage and bean casserole 102
    curried sweet potato and coconut 86
    feta and spinach lasagne 158–61
    fish pie 148
    and goats cheese hand pies 55
sweetcorn
    and cheese fritters 31
    courgette and sweetcorn muffins 57

T

tagine: Moroccan lamb tagine with couscous 121
tomatoes
    easy tomato relish 31
    roast tomato and red pepper soup 84
tortillas
    huevos rancheros 33
    Mexican beef fajitas 130
    red pepper and black bean enchiladas 162
totally tropical smoothie 94
turkey: quick meatballs on a sub roll with tomato sauce 134

V

veggie bolognaise 110

W

waffles, cheesy potato 36

Y

yoghurt: frozen yoghurt bark 181

MICHAEL JOSEPH

UK | USA | Canada | Ireland | Australia
India | New Zealand | South Africa

Penguin Michael Joseph, Penguin Random House UK, One Embassy Gardens, 8 Viaduct Gardens, London SW11 7BW

penguin.co.uk

global.penguinrandomhouse.com

First published 2025
003

Text copyright © Lou Robbie, 2025
Photography copyright © Ella Miller, 2025
Additional symbol illustration © Shutterstock, 2025

The moral right of the author has been asserted

Penguin Random House values and supports copyright. Copyright fuels creativity, encourages diverse voices, promotes freedom of expression and supports a vibrant culture. Thank you for purchasing an authorized edition of this book and for respecting intellectual property laws by not reproducing, scanning or distributing any part of it by any means without permission. You are supporting authors and enabling Penguin Random House to continue to publish books for everyone. No part of this book may be used or reproduced in any manner for the purpose of training artificial intelligence technologies or systems.

In accordance with Article 4(3) of the DSM Directive 2019/790, Penguin Random House expressly reserves this work from the text and data mining exception.

Set in Nerds Grotesk and Maison Neue

Colour reproduction by Altaimage Ltd
Printed and bound in Germany by
Mohn Media GmbH.

With design assistance from Gail Jones and Georgie Hewitt

The authorized representative in the EEA is Penguin Random House Ireland, Morrison Chambers, 32 Nassau Street, Dublin, D02 YH68.

A CIP catalogue record for this book is available from the British Library

ISBN: 9-780-241-73885-6

Penguin Random House is committed to a sustainable future for our business, our readers and our planet. This book is made from Forest Stewardship Council® certified paper.